THE BOOK OF

ROASTING

ROASTING

JEANETTE EGAN

HPBooks

CONTENTS

INTRODUCTION

Roasting is often associated with festive times such as holidays or special occasions. Nothing is more impressive for a special meal than a large standing rib roast (page 12) or a holiday turkey (page 39). Roasting is generally thought of as something to be done when plenty of time is available for cooking. However, roasting need not be merely reserved for holidays, guests or special events. With the availability of smaller roasts and the use of high- speed, high-temperature roasting, one can plan a quick-roasted meal during the week. Good choices for speedy roasting are boneless loin roasts, which can be cut to any weight, pork tenderloin, or chicken breasts. High-temperature roasting will give you sweet, caramelized vegetables in 10 minutes. Compared to steamed vegetables, roasted ones are bursting with flavor. Adding vegetables to the roasting pan along with the meat or chicken is an easy way to prepare a complete meal in the oven.

Even a fruit dessert can be prepared in about 10 minutes in your oven, then topped with an easy sauce, either one you make or purchase, or served with ice cream. Take advantage of seasonal fruits and adapt the recipes to what is available.

Roasted leftovers make delicious salads (pages 20, 38, and 48) and soup (page 21). The next time you prepare a weekend roast, plan on cooking a large enough roast for "overs" to make easy dinners during the week, or lunchtime sandwiches.

EQUIPMENT
Roasting doesn't require much in the way of special equipment but there are some basic items that will ensure a better product. All the roasts in this book were prepared in a standard, not convection, oven. The following equipment is suggested to make roasting easier.

Roasting pan: A good-quality, large, heavy roasting pan with sturdy handles is one of the essential pieces of equipment you should purchase. The pan should be about 17 x 12 x 3 inches. If the pan is too thin, the food

will stick and tend to burn, especially at the higher temperatures used for some of the meats and vegetables. Thinner pans will also burn the drippings and make them unsuitable for use in making pan sauces. It is helpful to have another smaller heavy roasting pan that can be used for roasting fruits or smaller amounts of vegetables. Roasting pans are available with a non-stick finish for easier clean-up.

Roasting racks: It is helpful to have both a V-shaped and a flat roasting rack. The V-shaped rack is used to hold large roasts and whole poultry. The flat rack is for smaller roasts, pork tenderloin, poultry pieces, or smaller items. Some roasting racks are adjustable and can be used either flat or V-shaped. The racks hold the food away from the bottom of the pan and allow the fat to drip into the roasting pan. They will also prevent a larger roast from becoming too brown on the bottom. Racks are available with non-stick finishes, which will make clean-up easier.

Thermometers: A thermometer is essential if you are doing high temperature roasting, because a roast can be overcooked in just a few minutes. While a thermometer is not as essential when roasting at lower temperatures (350F/180C) or below, it is a useful tool to ensure that the food is cooked to the temperature you desire. There are several different kinds of thermometers that can be used when roasting meats and poultry.

A standard meat thermometer is inserted into the meat or poultry at the beginning of roasting time. An instant-read thermometer is inserted into the food when it is removed from the oven; start checking 10 to 20 minutes, depending on the size of the roast, before the suggested cooking time is completed. An instant-read thermometer should never be left in the meat while it is still in the oven. The final choice, and my favorite, even though it is the more expensive, is a digital thermometer probe - a metal probe that is inserted into the food before it is placed into the oven. A metal wire leads out of the oven into the digital thermometer. The temperature of the roast is always displayed so it is easy to check the roasting progress. There

is usually an alarm setting that beeps when the roast has reached the desired set temperature. Some digital probes are also timers; others will even tell you the oven temperature, as well as the temperature of the food.

Because the actual temperature in your oven can vary widely from the temperature one sets on the dial or digital indicator, it is a good idea to routinely check your oven temperature with an oven thermometer and adjust the oven temperature setting accordingly, up or down to give you the actual temperature you are looking for.

Timers: In addition to a thermometer, it is helpful to set a timer, especially if you are using a meat or instant-read thermometer, as oven temperatures and roasts do vary. The timer should be set to remind you to check the roast 10 to 20 minutes before the time given in the recipe directions to ensure you are not overcooking the meat.

ACCESSORIES

In addition to the roasting equipment mentioned above, it is useful to have some accessories.

Carving tools: A sharp, long slicing knife and a sturdy sharp fork will make slicing roasts easier.

Heat-resistant silicone spatula: A heat-resistant spatula is useful for stirring roasting vegetables, because it will not tear or cut the vegetables as easily as a spoon and it will not damage a non-stick surface. Do not use a standard plastic spatula because the high heat will melt it.

Heavy-duty foil: To make clean-up easier, the roasting pan can be lined with aluminum foil. This is especially important if the pan does not have a non-stick surface.

BASIC TECHNIQUES

Roasting can be done using either dry heat or moist heat. Dry roasting, the type covered here, uses the more tender cuts of meats, poultry, and vegetables that benefit from the browning and caramelization (browning of the sugars) that occurs while the food is in the oven. The roast is usually uncovered during the cooking process, the food is not immersed in water, and the cooking period is shorter than for moist or pot roasting.

High-temperature roasting: One of the latest roasting techniques is using high oven temperatures - above 450F (230C). High temperatures tend to cause more shrinkage in meats and poultry, but it reduces the cooking time dramatically and creates a wonderful dark crust or skin. There may be some smoke from the oven and the roasts will splatter on the oven walls. As a precaution, you might want to temporarily remove your kitchen smoke detector and turn on the exhaust fan before opening the oven door. If you plan on using the drippings for a pan sauce, add a little water to the bottom of the roasting pan if they are getting too brown.

For some roasts, a higher oven temperature is used at the beginning of the roasting time and then the temperature is reduced to moderate for the remainder of the roasting time.

High-temperature roasting is particularly suited for smaller, tender beef roasts, vegetables, fish, and shellfish.

Moderate-temperature roasting: This is the standard method of roasting poultry, beef, lamb, and pork at temperatures between 300 and 350F (150 and 175C). The lower roasting temperature reduces shrinkage but does not give a brown crust, especially with smaller roasts. These can be browned on the stovetop before placing them in the oven or they can be broiled for a few minutes after the roasting is completed if a browner surface is desired. Moderate roasting temperatures are the best to use for flavorful, less tender cuts of beef such as eye of round or rump. The roasts will be more tender and moist than ones roasted at higher temperatures. In addition, some cooks suggest low-temperature roasting at 250F (120C), but that technique is not used here, because of the longer time required.

Moderate-temperature roasting can be used for whole poultry for even cooking that will result in a tender bird without too much shrinkage.

FLAVORING AND SEASONING
Flavor can be added to roasts through the use of glazes, marinades, and rubs as well as the liberal use of fresh and dried herbs and spices, plus salt and freshly ground pepper. If using a glaze that contains some form of sugar on a roast that requires more than 30 minutes of roasting time, complete part of the roasting before adding the glaze to prevent burning it. A larger roast may need to be turned to glaze all the sides evenly. Cover the roast with foil if the roast browns too quickly.

Marinades are used to add flavor and to tenderize a less-tender cut. Tender roasts such as pork tenderloin and fish can be marinated for flavor only for a limited period of time, and never as long as overnight. Any meat or fish that is marinated for more than 30 minutes should be placed in the refrigerator to prevent the growth of harmful bacteria that may be present. Any marinade that has been used on raw meat, fish, or poultry should be brought to a boil before using it as a sauce.

Dry rubs are an easy way to season chicken, ribs, and other roasts. They can be made from a combination of spices (pages 88 to 89) or herbs. Remove the amount of the rub needed for a roast from the jar with a clean spoon, not your fingers, to avoid contaminating the remaining mixture. Rubs can be stored for several months. Besides adding flavor, they also make the roast more attractive by adding color and aiding in caramelizing the surface of the roast. Wet rubs are also used on some roasts.

The fat can be removed from the drippings, which can be used as the base for a delicious pan sauce. Sauces, chutneys and other condiments can be added.

Meats: Usually the more tender cuts of meat are roasted. For beef this includes the loin, rib eye, sirloin, and fillet, but less tender cuts are often the most flavorful and can be roasted if they are done so at moderate temperatures, roasted just to rare to medium doneness, and thinly sliced across the grain (muscle).

Leg and rack of lamb are both good choices for roasting. The leg is available whole or cut into smaller, more convenient, sometimes boned roasts. Pork loin, tenderloin, pork shoulder, and ham, or almost any cut of pork, can all be roasted. Pork can be coated with a dry rub or marinated for extra flavor.

Poultry: Rinse poultry with cold water and remove the excess fat. Pat the poultry dry before placing in the oven to ensure even browning. Season poultry with herbs, rubs, or glazes. Poultry can be roasted at either moderate- or high-oven temperatures. Let the cooked bird rest about 20 minutes before carving for more moist meat.

Fish and Shellfish: Fish usually requires about 10 minutes of roasting time per inch of thickness (measuring at the thickest part) in a 425 to 450F (220 to 230C) oven.

Vegetables: Cut vegetables into pieces of equal size to ensure that they will roast

evenly. Enough vegetables for four to six servings can be cooked in a large roasting pan. Toss the vegetables with about 1 tablespoon oil and 1 tablespoon water before roasting. The water reduces the amount of oil needed and the oil helps the vegetables brown. Vegetables can be seasoned before or after roasting. Roasted vegetables can be served as a side dish or added to soups or salads.

Fruits: Choose ripe but not overly soft fruits for roasting. Chop or slice into uniform pieces. Most fruits should be roasted at high oven temperatures for a short period of time for the best results.

DONENESS TESTS

Beef and lamb: Cook beef and lamb to 140F (60C) for rare, 160F (70C) for medium, and 170F (75C) for well done, depending on your personal preference. Some of the less tender cuts have the most flavor, but are better if roasted to no more than medium. Remember that the larger the roast, the more the temperature will rise after the roast is removed from the oven. The temperature of a large roast may rise 10 to 15 degrees Fahrenheit or 10 degrees Celsius. Even the temperature of a small roast will rise about 5 degrees. Bone-in roasts will cook more quickly than a roast that has had the bones removed.

Pork: Cook until juices run clear and the thermometer registers 160 to 170F (70 to 75C). Very lean cuts of pork can be cooked to 150 to 155F (60 to 65C). Because today's pork has less fat than that

of several years ago, it can be dry and tough if overcooked.

Chicken: Cook whole chicken until the flesh is white, the juices run clear and the drumsticks move easily. A thermometer inserted into the thigh should register 180F (80C) and a thermometer in the breast should register 165 to 170F (75C). Cook chicken pieces until tender, cooked through, and until the flesh is no longer pink.

Duck and goose: Duck breasts are often served medium or rare, but the legs need to be cooked until well done. Because of the differences in cooking time, duck breasts are sometimes cooked separately. When cooking a whole duck, if you want to serve the breast rare or medium, remove the legs and return them to the oven for more roasting.

A goose is cooked until tender and the drumsticks move easily. Both ducks and geese are very fatty and the fat may need to be spooned off one or two times as it accumulates during roasting. Adding a little water to the roasting pan can keep the fat from becoming too hot and smoking.

Turkey: Cook a whole turkey until a thermometer inserted in the thigh registers 180 to 185F (80 to 85C) and the drumsticks can be moved easily. If a turkey has been stuffed, the temperature of the interior of the stuffing should reach 160F (70C). Cook a turkey breast until a thermometer registers 165 to 170F (75C).

Fish and shellfish: Fish should be cooked just until it begins to flake and the color changes from translucent to opaque. The exception to this rule is fresh tuna, which is often just cooked until the exterior changes color and the interior still has a reddish center. Shrimp should turn pink or start to curl into a circle. Scallops are very delicate and should be cooked just until they are white.

RIB EYE ROAST

1 (about 3lb) beef rib eye roast
salt and freshly ground pepper, to taste
CRANBERRY SAUCE:
1 medium apple, peeled and chopped
1 medium onion, chopped
1 cup cranberry or apple juice
1/4 cup red wine
1/4 cup sugar
3 cups fresh or frozen cranberries
1 teaspoon grated fresh ginger
2 teaspoons dry mustard

Preheat oven to 350F (180C). Pat roast dry and season with salt and pepper.

Place roast on a rack in a roasting pan. Roast about 40 minutes for rare, until a thermometer registers 140F (60C), or to desired doneness. To make sauce, bring apple, onion, juice, wine, and sugar to a boil over medium-high heat. Reduce heat to low and simmer until onion is tender, about 15 minutes, stirring occasionally. Stir in cranberries, ginger, and mustard. Cook until cranberries pop and mixture thickens, about 10 minutes.

Season with salt and pepper. Transfer to a food processor and pulse until coarsely pureed. Serve warm or at room temperature.

Serves 6

ROAST WITH VEGETABLES

1 (about 3lb) beef chuck roast, rib end (sometimes
  called cross-rib)
2 tablespoons light brown sugar
1 tablespoon balsamic vinegar
salt and freshly ground pepper, to taste
3 to 4 medium baking potatoes
5 carrots, peeled
2 medium onions
2 large portabello mushrooms
1 tablespoon olive oil

Preheat oven to 350F (180C). Pat roast dry
with paper towels. Combine brown sugar
and vinegar in a small bowl.

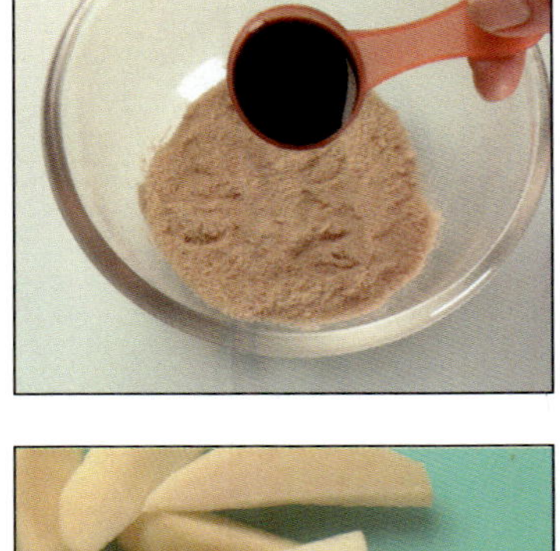

Rub sugar mixture into beef and season beef
with salt and pepper. Let stand while
preparing vegetables. Cut potatoes into
wedges. Cut each carrot into 3 pieces. Cut
onions into quarters. Wipe mushrooms with
a damp paper towel; cut into 8 wedges each.
Combine vegetables in a large bowl. Add
olive oil; toss to coat. Season with salt and
pepper.

Arrange vegetables in a large heavy roasting
pan. Place beef in a V-shaped rack over
vegetables. Roast about 1 hour for rare, until
a thermometer registers 140F (60C), or to
desired doneness, stirring vegetables
occasionally. (This is a very flavorful cut,
but it will be tough if cooked until well
done.) Let stand 5 to 10 minutes before
thinly slicing on the diagonal. Serve with
the vegetables.

Serves 6–8

PEPPERED ROAST

1 (about 4lb) beef rump or top round roast
2 tablespoons Dijon mustard
1 tablespoon honey
1 tablespoon olive oil
1 tablespoon whisky
1 teaspoon dried thyme
1 to 2 tablespoons freshly cracked black pepper, or
  to taste

Preheat oven to 350F (180C). Pat roast dry
with paper towels.

Combine mustard, honey, olive oil, whisky,
and thyme in a small bowl. Rub into beef.

Press cracked pepper evenly over beef. Place
beef in a V-shaped rack in a roasting pan.
Roast about 1½ hours for rare, until a
thermometer registers 140F (60C), or to
desired doneness. (This roast is best served
rare or medium.) Let stand 5 to 10 minutes
before thinly slicing on the diagonal.

Serves 8

RIB ROAST WITH SHERRY SAUCE

1 (6 to 7lb) beef standing rib roast
1 teaspoon dried thyme
salt and freshly ground pepper, to taste
SHERRY SAUCE:
1/2 cup dry Sherry
1 cup beef stock
1/4 cup Dijon mustard
1 tablespoon Worcestershire sauce
1 tablespoon cornstarch mixed with 2 tablespoons
  water
1/4 cup capers
3 teaspoons chopped fresh thyme, or 1 teaspoon
  dried

Preheat oven to 475F (245C).

Pat roast dry with paper towels. Place beef on a rack in a roasting pan. Season beef with thyme, salt, and pepper. Roast 15 minutes. Reduce oven temperature to 350F (180C). Roast about 1 1/2 hours for rare, until a thermometer in center of roast registers 125F (50C), or to desired doneness (internal temperature will rise 15 degrees F or 10 degrees C during standing). Place roast on a platter and cover with foil. Let stand 30 minutes before carving.

To make sauce, discard fat from pan or reserve for Herbed Yorkshire Pudding (page 16). Add Sherry and bring to a boil over high heat, scraping up browned bits. Transfer to a saucepan. Stir in stock, mustard, Worcestershire sauce, cornstarch mixture, capers, and thyme. Cook over medium heat, stirring, until slightly thickened and mixture is boiling. Season with salt and pepper. Carve roast and serve with sauce.

Serves 8–10

– HERBED YORKSHIRE PUDDING –

1/4 cup drippings from roast (page 00) or vegetable oil
1 1/4 cups unbleached all-purpose flour
1/8 teaspoon salt
1 tablespoon chopped fresh chives
1 1/2 teaspoons fresh thyme leaves, or 1/2 teaspoon dried
2 eggs
1 cup milk

Preheat oven to 425F (220C). Add 1 teaspoon of the drippings to each of 12 muffin cups or ramekins. Place in the oven to heat while making the batter.

Combine flour, salt, chives, and thyme in a mixing bowl. Beat eggs and milk together in another bowl and add to flour mixture. Beat well.

Ladle batter equally into muffin cups, filling about halfway. Bake 30 to 35 minutes, until puffed, golden brown, and firm to the touch. Serve immediately.

Makes 12

BEEF & PEAR SALAD

1/4 cup mayonnaise
1/4 cup plain yogurt
1 tablespoon Dijon mustard
1 tablespoon lemon juice
2 tablespoons snipped chives
milk, as needed
salt and freshly ground pepper, to taste
2 red Bartlett pears
2 cups (about 8oz) julienned roasted beef (page 12 or 13)
4 to 6 cups baby spinach
1/4 cup crumbled blue cheese
1/4 cup walnuts, toasted

Combine mayonnaise, yogurt, mustard, lemon juice, and chives in a small bowl. Add enough milk to make a pouring consistency. Season with salt and pepper. Remove stems from pears. Cut each pear in half from stem end to blossom end. Remove cores. Slice unpeeled pears into 1/4-inch slices.

Divide spinach among 4 plates. Alternately arrange pears and beef over spinach. Sprinkle with blue cheese and walnuts. Drizzle with dressing.

Serves 4

— BEEF WITH PORT MARINADE —

1 (2 to 3lb) beef eye of round roast
$^1/_4$ cup white port
2 tablespoons olive oil
1 tablespoon Worcestershire sauce
2 bay leaves
1 large clove garlic, minced
2 thyme sprigs
1 tablespoon whole peppercorns
$^3/_4$ cup beef stock
1 tablespoon tomato paste
1 tablespoon cornstarch mixed with 2 tablespoons
  water (optional)

Rinse beef and pat dry with paper towels. Place in a large resealable bag.

Combine port, olive oil, Worcestershire sauce, bay leaves, garlic, thyme, and peppercorns in a small bowl. Pour over beef in bag, seal and turn to coat. Marinate in the refrigerator 2 to 3 hours, or overnight, turning occasionally. Preheat oven to 425F (220C). Remove beef from marinade. Strain marinade and reserve. Place beef on a rack in a roasting pan. Roast about 1 hour, 15 minutes, until a thermometer inserted in the thickest part registers 140F (55C) for rare, or to desired doneness.

Transfer roast to a platter. Spoon off fat from drippings and place pan over medium heat. Add stock to pan and bring to a boil, scraping up browned bits. Stir in reserved marinade. Boil, stirring, until slightly reduced. For a thicker sauce, stir in cornstarch mixture; cook, stirring, until bubbly and thickened. Slice roast and serve sauce on the side.

Serves 6

— BEEF WITH MUSHROOMS —

1 (3¹/₂ to 4lb) beef loin top sirloin
salt and freshly ground pepper, to taste
1 tablespoon butter
1 tablespoon chopped shallot
6oz fresh mushrooms, sliced
1¹/₂ cups beef stock
1¹/₂ teaspoons dried mushroom powder (see below)
¹/₂ cup heavy cream

Preheat oven to 425F (220C). Season roast with salt and pepper. Place beef on a rack in a roasting pan.

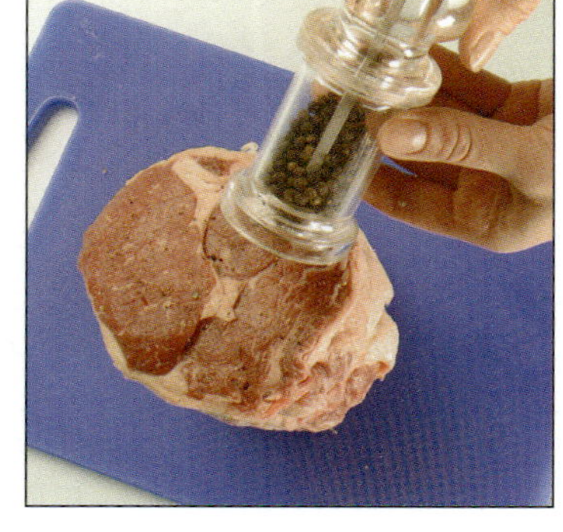

Roast about 1 hour, 35 minutes, until a thermometer inserted in the thickest part registers 140F (55C) for rare, or to desired doneness. Melt butter in a skillet over medium heat. Add shallot and sauté until softened. Add mushrooms and sauté until softened and juices evaporate. Transfer roast to a platter.

Spoon off fat from drippings and place pan over medium heat. Add stock to pan and bring to a boil. Add stock and mushroom powder to mushrooms. Boil, stirring, until slightly reduced. Stir in cream; cook, stirring, until hot. Season. Slice roast and serve sauce on the side.

Serves 8

NOTE: To make mushroom powder, grind dried mushrooms in a mini food processor, blender, or spice grinder until powdered.

BEEF & NOODLE SALAD

8oz rice noodles
1 cup julienned red bell pepper
$^1/_2$ cup julienned carrots
$^1/_4$ cup sliced green onions
2 cups (8oz) julienned roasted beef (page 12 or 13)
2 tablespoons peanut oil
1 tablespoon seasoned rice vinegar
1 tablespoon black bean garlic sauce
$^1/_4$ teaspoon crushed red pepper, or to taste
3 cups packed baby spinach

Break noodle bundle into about 3-inch pieces. Cook according to package directions; drain. Transfer to a bowl.

Add bell pepper, carrots, green onions, and beef to noodles. Combine oil, rice vinegar, black bean garlic sauce, and crushed red pepper in a small bowl. Pour over noodle mixture and toss to combine.

Arrange spinach on 4 serving plates. Arrange noodle mixture over spinach.

Serves 4

VARIATION: Toss noodles with the vegetables. Top each salad with beef. Drizzle dressing over the top.

── SOUTHEAST ASIAN SOUP ──

10 cups canned beef broth (about four 14^1/$_2$-oz cans)
2 stalks lemon grass, chopped
5 slices fresh ginger
3 cloves garlic, sliced
2 star anise
2 tablespoons fish sauce (nuoc nam or nam pla)
1 (9 to 12oz) package fresh udon noodles or fresh
  linguine
4 green onions, thinly sliced
4 serrano chiles, thinly sliced
4 tablespoons each chopped fresh cilantro, basil, and
  mint
2 limes, cut into wedges
2 cups (8oz) julienned roast beef (page 12 or 13)
4 cups bean sprouts

Bring broth, lemon grass, ginger, garlic, star anise, and fish sauce to a boil in a large saucepan. Reduce heat and simmer 20 minutes. Strain broth into a bowl; discard seasonings. Cook noodles in large pot of boiling salted water until tender but firm to the bite. Drain; rinse with cold water. Arrange green onions, chiles, herbs, and lime wedges on a platter.

Bring strained broth, beef, noodles, and bean sprouts to a boil. Divide among 6 bowls. Add green onions, chiles, and herbs as desired. Serve with lime wedges.

Serves 6

– ASIAN-FLAVORED LAMB RACK –

2 (about 1¹/₂lb) racks of lamb
¹/₄ cup fresh cilantro
2 tablespoons mango chutney
1 teaspoon grated fresh ginger
1 garlic clove, minced
¹/₂ cup bread crumbs
¹/₂ teaspoon five-spice powder
1 tablespoon olive oil

Preheat oven to 400F (205C). Place lamb, bones side down, in a roasting pan.

Pulse cilantro, chutney, ginger, garlic, crumbs, and five-spice powder in a blender or mini food processor until combined. Add oil and process to a paste.

Spread paste evenly over the lamb. Roast about 20 minutes for rare, until thermometer registers 140F (60C), or to desired doneness. Cut each rack into 2 portions.

Serves 4

GREEK STYLE LAMB

1 (3lb) deboned sirloin half lamb leg
3 cloves garlic, slivered
1/4 cup olive oil
2 tablespoons lemon juice
1 tablespoon grated lemon zest
1 teaspoon dried leaf oregano
1 teaspoon dried rosemary
1 teaspoon dried mint
1 teaspoon salt
1 teaspoon coarsely ground pepper

Preheat oven to 350F (180C). Remove excess fat from lamb. With the sharp point of a knife, cut small slits in the lamb. Insert garlic into the slits.

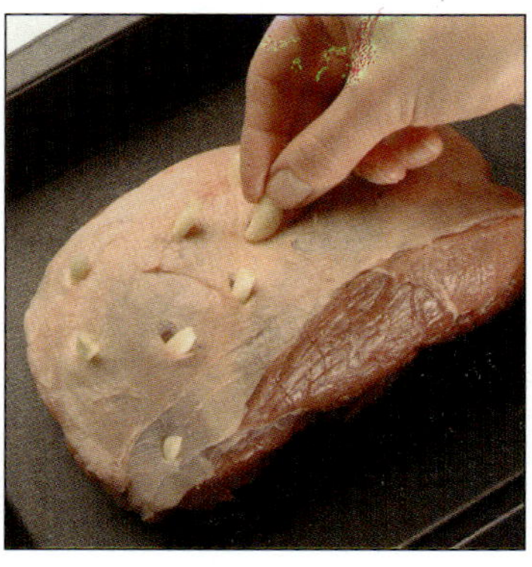

Combine oil, lemon juice, zest, herbs, salt, and pepper in a small bowl. Rub mixture over lamb.

Place lamb in a V-shaped rack in a large roasting pan. Roast about 1 hour for rare, until a thermometer inserted in thickest part registers 140F (60C), or to desired doneness. Let stand about 10 minutes before slicing.

Serves 6–8

MIDDLE EASTERN LAMB

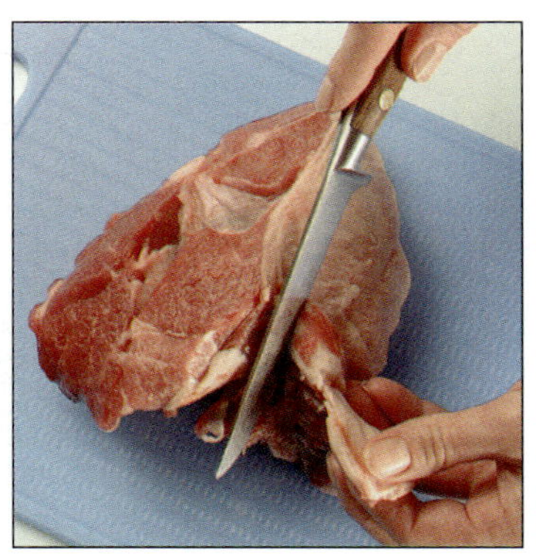

1 (3lb) sirloin half lamb leg with bone
1/4 cup olive oil
2 large cloves garlic, minced
1 teaspoon ground cumin
1 teaspoon ground coriander
1/2 teaspoon sweet paprika
1/4 teaspoon ground cinnamon
1/4 teaspoon ginger
1 teaspoon coarsely ground pepper
1/2 teaspoon salt

Preheat oven to 350F (180C). Remove excess fat from lamb.

Combine oil, garlic, spices, and salt in a small bowl. Rub mixture over lamb.

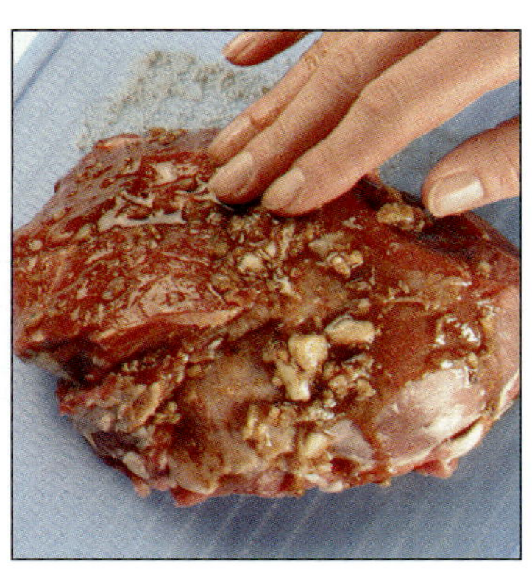

Place lamb in a V-shaped rack in a large roasting pan. Roast 45 to 60 minutes for rare, until a thermometer inserted in the thickest part registers 140F (60C), or to desired doneness. Let stand about 10 minutes before slicing.

Serves 6–8

— PORK WITH MIMOSA SAUCE —

1 (6 to 7lb) rack of pork roast (about 8 ribs)
salt and freshly ground pepper, to taste
2 teaspoons minced fresh rosemary
2 large cloves garlic, minced
$^1/_2$ cup fresh sour orange juice or $^1/_4$ cup each sweet
  orange juice and lemon juice
1 tablespoon grated orange zest
$^1/_2$ cup champagne or dry white wine
1 tablespoon cornstarch mixed with $^1/_4$ cup water or
  chicken broth

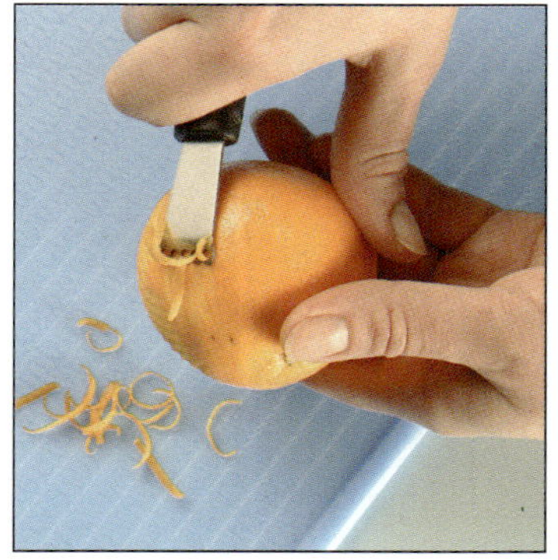

Preheat oven to 450F (220C). Season with
salt and pepper. Rub with rosemary and
garlic. Place in a roasting pan, bones side
down. Roast about 1 hour, 30 minutes, until
thermometer inserted in thickest part
registers 160F (70C) and juices run clear.
Let stand 10 minutes before carving.

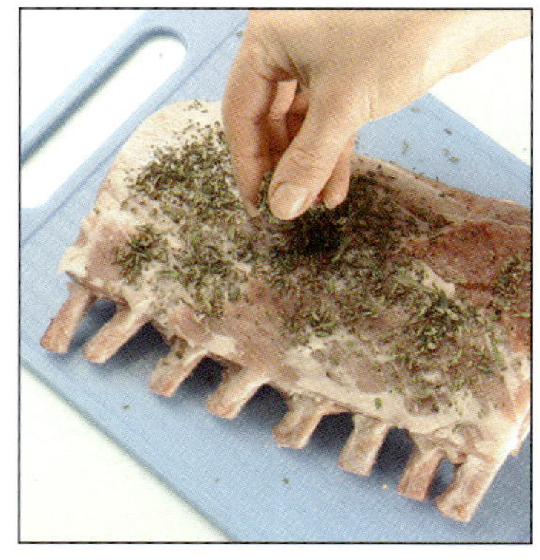

Skim fat from pan juices. Place pan over
high heat; stir in orange juice, stirring to
loosen browned bits. Boil until juice is
reduced by half. Stir in zest, champagne,
and cornstarch mixture; cook, stirring, until
thickened. Season with salt and pepper.
Serve with pork.

Serves 8

CARIBBEAN PORK TENDERLOIN

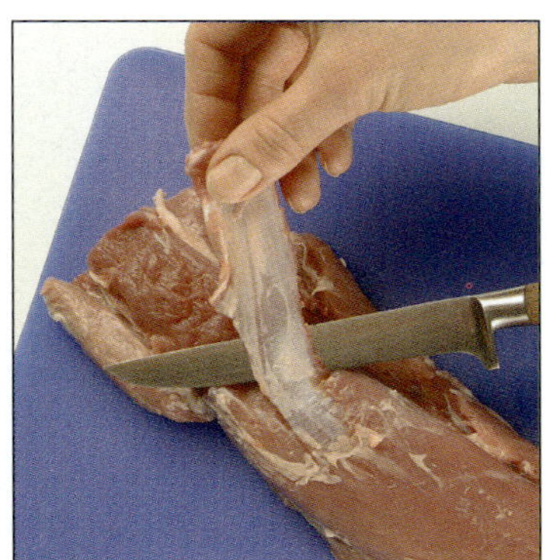

2 (about 2lb) pork tenderloins, silverskin removed
Jerk Rub (page 89)
1 cup chopped papaya
1 cup chopped avocado
1/4 cup finely chopped red bell pepper
1 tablespoon minced green onion
2 teaspoons minced jalapeño chile, or to taste
2 tablespoons lemon juice

Preheat oven to 400F (205C). Rub pork all over with Jerk Rub. Place in a roasting pan. Roast about 20 minutes, or until a thermometer in the thickest part of the pork registers 150 to 155F (65 to 70C).

Meanwhile, combine papaya, avocado, bell pepper, green onion, chile, and lemon juice in a medium bowl. Let stand 10 minutes for flavors to blend. Let pork rest 10 minutes. Cut pork into about 1/2-inch-thick slices. Serve papaya salsa on the side.

Serves 4–6

PORK TENDERLOIN WITH APPLES

1 large onion, thinly sliced
1 teaspoon dried sage
1 tablespoon salt
1 tablespoon freshly ground pepper
2 (about 2lb) pork tenderloins, silverskin removed
1 tablespoon olive oil
2 apples, cored and thinly sliced crosswise
1/2 teaspoon ground cinnamon
2 tablespoons honey
1/2 cup frozen apple juice concentrate, thawed
1/4 cup chicken broth
1/4 cup heavy cream
salt and freshly ground pepper, to taste

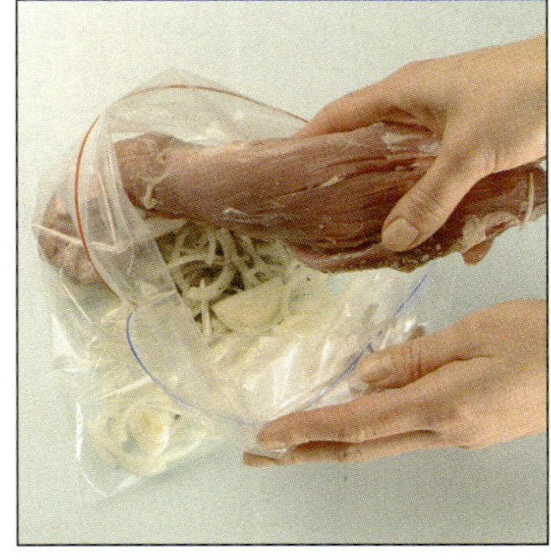

Combine onion, sage, salt, and pepper in a plastic resealable bag. Add pork and cover with onion mixture. Refrigerate 2 to 3 hours. Preheat oven to 400F (205C). Remove pork from marinade, discarding marinade. Pat pork dry with paper towels. Brown pork in oil in a large skillet over high heat. Arrange apples in roasting pan. Sprinkle with cinnamon and drizzle with honey. Place pork on apples. Roast about 20 minutes, or until a thermometer in the thickest part of the pork registers 150 to 155F (65 to 70C), and apples are tender.

Remove pork and apples to a serving dish. Place pan over high heat. Stir in juice, broth, and cream, scraping bottom of pan. Simmer until reduced by about half. Season with salt and pepper. Cut pork into about 1/2-inch-thick slices and serve with apples and sauce.

Serves 4–6

SAUSAGE-STUFFED PORK

4oz bulk pork sausage
1/4 finely chopped onion
1/4 cup chopped celery
4oz fresh mushrooms, chopped
1 cup cooked brown or wild rice
1/4 cup pine nuts, toasted
2 tablespoons dried zante currants
2 teaspoons dried thyme
1/8 teaspoon cayenne pepper
2 (about 2lb) pork tenderloins, silverskin removed
1 teaspoon dried thyme
salt and freshly ground pepper, to taste

Cook sausage, stirring to break up, over medium heat until browned.

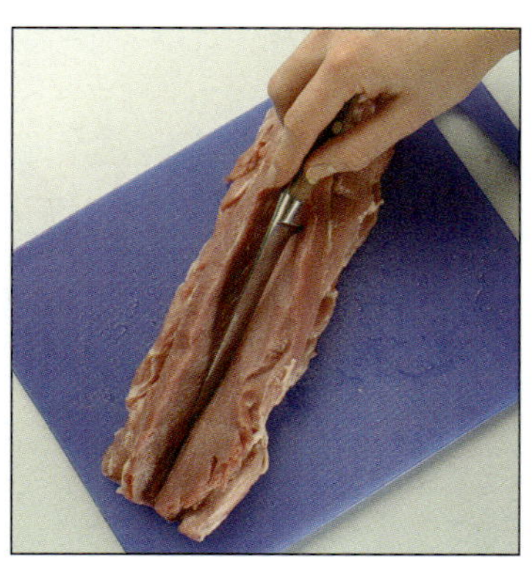

Add onion, celery, and mushrooms; sauté until tender. Transfer to a bowl and stir in rice, pine nuts, currants, 1 teaspoon of the thyme, and cayenne. Preheat oven to 350F (180C). Butterfly pork tenderloins by cutting lengthwise, leaving 1/4 inch to connect the two sections. Pound until flattened to about 1/4-inch thickness. Lay one tenderloin on work surface. Mound stuffing on tenderloin, leaving edges clear.

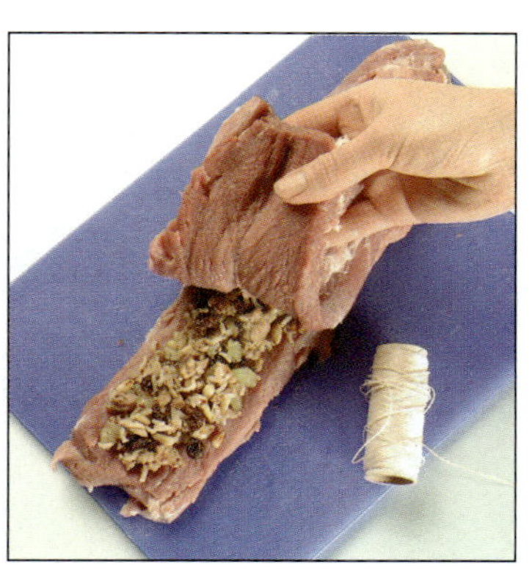

Place remaining tenderloin over stuffing. Tie with kitchen string about every 2 inches to hold stuffing in place. Season with thyme, salt, and pepper. Place in roasting pan. Roast about 40 minutes, until a thermometer in the pork and stuffing registers 150 to 155F (65 to 70C). Let rest 5 minutes. Cut into about 1/2-inch-thick slices.

Serves 4–6

— PORK WITH CHERRY SAUCE —

1 (3lb) pork loin roast
salt and freshly ground pepper, to taste
3/4 cup cherry syrup from cherries
1/4 cup Marsala
1 tablespoon cornstarch mixed with 2 tablespoons
    water
1/2 cup drained, canned dark sweet cherries in light
    syrup
1 tablespoon grated orange zest

Preheat oven to 350F (180C). Season pork with salt and pepper. Place on a rack in a heavy roasting pan.

Roast about 1 hour, until a thermometer inserted in thickest part registers 160F (70C), or to desired doneness. Let stand about 10 minutes before slicing. Meanwhile, combine cherry syrup and Marsala in a saucepan over medium heat. Stir in cornstarch mixture. Bring to a boil, stirring constantly. Cook until thickened.

Stir in cherries and orange zest. Serve with pork.

Serves 6

- PORK CUBES, ONION, & GARLIC -

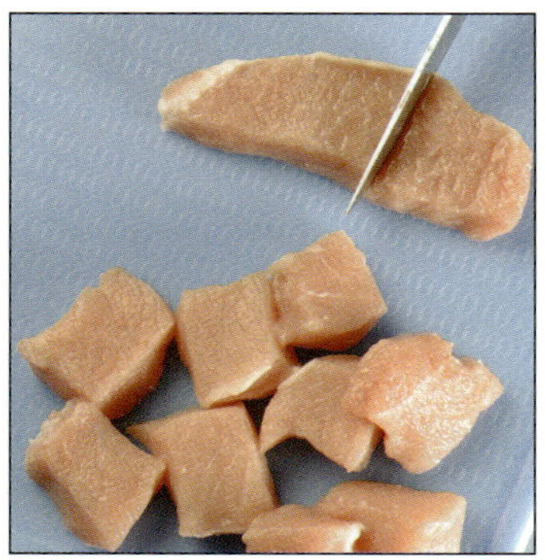

2lb lean boneless pork
2 cups chopped onions
2 large cloves garlic, chopped
2 tablespoons frozen tropical juice concentrate
  (passion fruit or guava), thawed
1 tablespoon balsamic vinegar
1 tablespoon fresh thyme or 1 1/2 teaspoons dried
  thyme
1/2 teaspoon dried rosemary
2 bay leaves
salt and freshly ground pepper, to taste

Preheat oven to 400F (205C). Cut pork into
1-inch cubes.

Combine pork, onions, and garlic in a large
bowl. Add juice concentrate, vinegar,
thyme, rosemary, and bay leaves. Season
with salt and pepper. Toss to combine.

Transfer pork mixture to a greased large and
heavy roasting pan. Roast in middle of oven
about 30 minutes, until pork is cooked
through and onions are tender, stirring two
times. Discard bay leaves. Serve in tortillas
or pita pockets, or with noodles and
vegetables.

Serves 4

VEAL WITH MUSHROOM SAUCE

about 2³/4lb veal loin, preferably naturally raised
salt and freshly ground pepper
2 thin slices pork fat or (streaky) bacon
1 tablespoon butter
4oz fresh shiitake mushrooms, thinly sliced
¹/2 cup dry white wine
¹/2 cup heavy cream
1 teaspoon minced fresh tarragon or ¹/2 teaspoon
  dried

Preheat oven to 350F (180C). Season veal
with salt and pepper. Arrange fat over veal
and tie in place with kitchen twine. Place
veal in a heavy roasting pan.

Roast about 1¹/2 hours, until a thermometer
registers 150F (65C). Melt butter in a skillet
over medium heat. Add mushrooms and
sauté until softened and juices
evaporate.

Transfer veal to a cutting board. Skim off
excess fat from drippings. Stir in wine to
loosen browned bits and simmer on stovetop
until reduced by half. Add wine, cream, and
tarragon to mushrooms. Season with salt
and pepper. Slice veal and serve with sauce
on the side.

Serves 6

— VENISON & CHIPTOLE BUTTER —

1 (3lb) venison loin roast
2 tablespoons olive oil
salt and freshly ground pepper, to taste
CHIPTOLE BUTTER:
2 canned chiptole chiles in adobe sauce
$1/2$ cup (4oz) butter, softened
2 tablespoons brandy
1 teaspoon fresh thyme or $1/2$ teaspoon dried

Preheat oven to 400F (205C). Pat roast dry with paper towels. Heat oil in a large heavy skillet over high heat. Add venison to skillet and brown on all sides.

Transfer venison to a rack in a roasting pan. Season with salt and pepper. Roast about 30 minutes for rare, until a thermometer registers 140F (60C), or to desired doneness. (Because venison is a very lean meat, it should never be roasted until well done.)

To make the butter, pulse chiles in a blender or small food processor until pureed. Add butter, brandy, and thyme. Pulse until combined. Mixture can be formed into a log and chilled or served soft. Remove venison from oven and let stand 5 to 10 minutes. Slice and serve with butter.

Serves 6

‑ SOUTHWESTERN RIBS & CORN ‑

6lb pork back ribs (2 racks)
Southwestern Rub (page 88)
CORN WITH LIME BUTTER:
4 to 6 ears of corn with husks
1/4 cup butter or margarine, softened
1 tablespoon lime juice
2 teaspoons grated lime zest
1 teaspoon mild chile powder (optional)

Preheat oven to 350F (180C). Sprinkle about 1 tablespoon rub on each side of ribs; rub in. Arrange ribs on a rack in a large roasting pan. Roast ribs about 30 minutes.

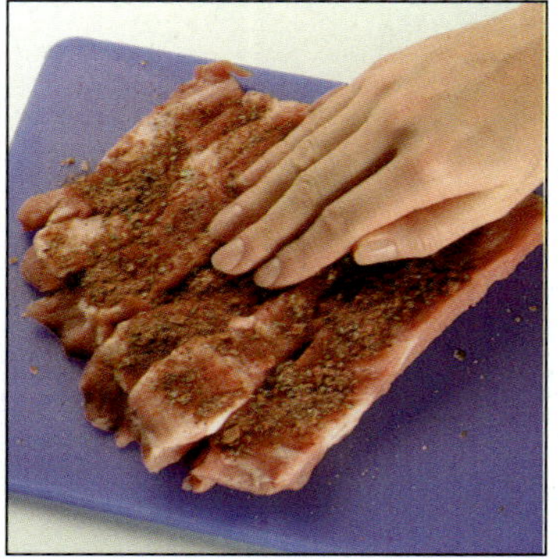

Meanwhile, remove outer leaves from corn and trim ends, leaving 2 or 3 inner layers. Rinse corn in cold water. Place corn directly on oven rack in oven with ribs. Roast corn and ribs 30 minutes, until corn husks begin to brown, the milk in the corn kernels has set, the ribs are tender, and the rib juices are clear when pieced with a knife point.

To make the lime butter, combine butter, lime juice, zest, and chile powder (if using) in a small bowl. Remove corn from the oven and cool slightly. Remove husks and silks from corn and place on a serving plate. Spread corn with lime butter. Transfer ribs to a cutting board. Cut into one-rib pieces and serve with corn.

Serves 4–6

— SAUSAGE, PEPPERS, & ONIONS —

1 large red bell pepper
1 large green bell pepper
1 large onion
1 large clove garlic, minced
1 teaspoon dried oregano
1 teaspoon dried basil
1 tablespoon olive oil
4 cooked Italian sausages (see Note below)
polenta or rice, to serve

Preheat oven to 450F (230C). Cut bell peppers into halves lengthwise. Remove cores and seeds. Cut lengthwise into 1/2-inch-wide strips.

Cut onion in half lengthwise; cut halves crosswise into slices and separate. Add bell peppers, onion, garlic, herbs, and olive oil to a large bowl; toss to combine. Transfer to a large rimmed baking sheet. Roast about 5 minutes, until vegetables are softened.

Cut sausages diagonally into 3 or 4 pieces. Add to vegetables and stir to mix. Roast 10 minutes, until sausages are hot and vegetables are tender. Serve on polenta.

Serves 4

NOTE: If sausages are uncooked, cut into 3 or 4 pieces. Omit olive oil and add sausages to roasting pan with vegetables for the full roasting time.

HAM & PINEAPPLE SALSA

$^1/_2$ cup frozen pineapple juice concentrate, thawed
$^1/_2$ teaspoon ground ginger
1 (6lb) fully cooked ham with bone
1 cup finely chopped fresh pineapple
1 cup finely chopped fresh mango
$^1/_4$ cup finely chopped green bell pepper
$^1/_4$ cup raisins
2 tablespoons chopped red onion
2 tablespoons seasoned rice vinegar
1 tablespoon minced fresh ginger

Preheat oven to 350F (180C). Combine pineapple juice concentrate and ground ginger in a small bowl.

Place ham in a rack in a heavy roasting pan. Brush with some of the juice mixture. Roast 1 hour; brush with remaining juice. Roast for a further hour, until a thermometer inserted in the thickest part registers 140F (60C). Let stand about 10 minutes before slicing.

Combine pineapple, mango, bell pepper, raisins, onion, vinegar, and ginger in a medium bowl. Let stand 10 minutes for flavors to blend.

Serves 4–6, with some ham left over

GLAZED TURKEY BREAST

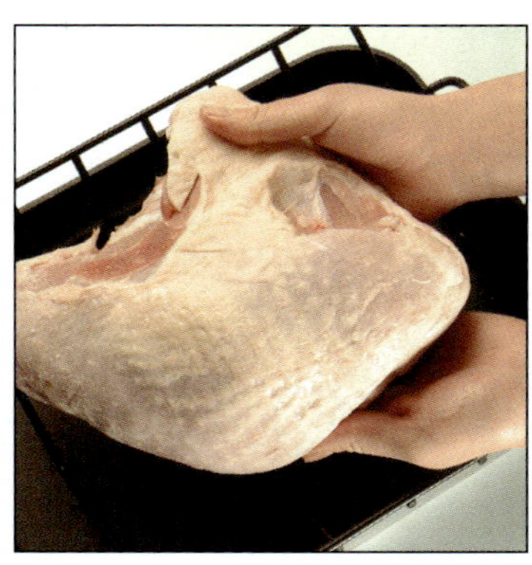

1 (about 3lb) half turkey breast with bone
1/4 cup orange marmalade
1/2 teaspoon ground cinnamon
1/4 teaspoon ground allspice
1/4 teaspoon ground ginger
1/2 teaspoon salt

Preheat oven to 350F (180C). Rinse turkey in cold water and pat dry with paper towels. Place turkey in a V-shaped rack in a heavy roasting pan. Roast for 30 minutes.

Combine orange marmalade, spices, and salt in a small bowl. Brush some of the mixture over the turkey.

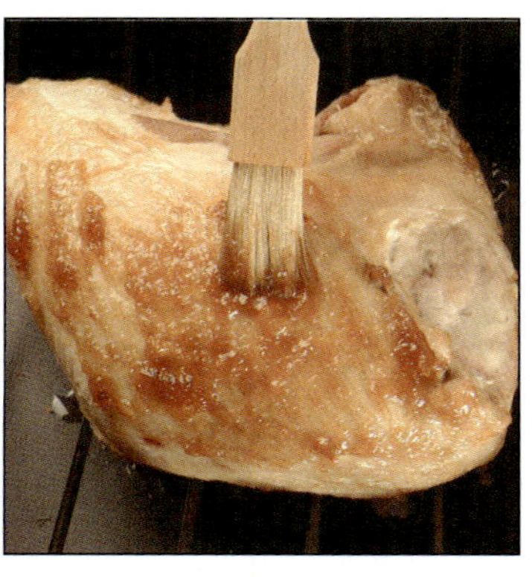

Roast for 15 minutes; brush with remaining marmalade mixture. Roast about 20 minutes, until a thermometer inserted in thickest part registers 170F (75C). Remove turkey from pan. Let stand about 10 minutes before slicing.

Serves 6

NOTE: Leftover turkey can be used for sandwiches or salads (see page 38)

TURKEY & BLACKBERRY SAUCE

1 (3lb) rolled turkey breast
1 teaspoon dried thyme
salt and freshly ground pepper, to taste
$^1/_2$ cup chicken stock
1 tablespoon butter
1 tablespoon chopped shallot
$^1/_2$ cup seedless blackberry jam
2 tablespoons white wine vinegar
1 cup fresh or frozen blackberries (optional)

Preheat oven to 350F (180C). Rinse turkey in cold water and pat dry with paper towels. Sprinkle with thyme and season with salt and pepper.

Place turkey in a V-shaped rack in a heavy roasting pan. Roast about 1$^1/_2$ hours, until a thermometer inserted in thickest part registers 170F (75C). Remove turkey from pan. Let stand about 10 minutes before slicing.

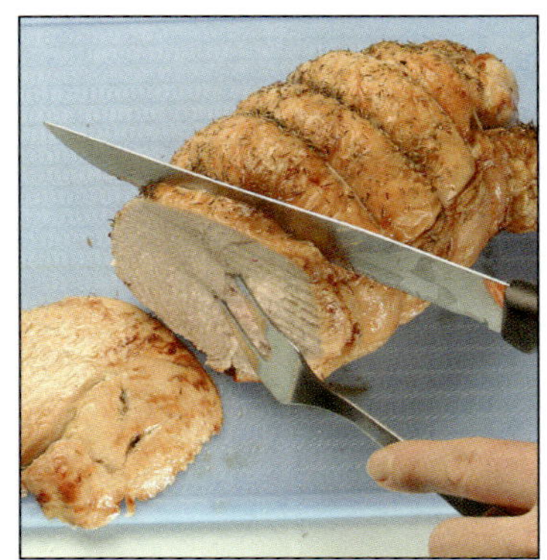

Stir in stock to loosen browned bits. Melt butter in a saucepan over medium heat. Add shallot and sauté until softened. Stir in stock from roasting pan, jam, and vinegar. Season with salt and pepper. Stir in blackberries (if using). Slice turkey and serve with sauce on the side.

Serves 6

ROASTED TURKEY SALAD

1/2 cup olive or canola oil
1/4 cup fresh lemon juice
2 teaspoons Dijon mustard
1 teaspoon dried oregano
1/2 teaspoon dried marjoram
1 clove garlic, minced (optional)
salt and freshly ground pepper, to taste
1/2 cucumber
1 avocado, diced
1 cup cherry tomatoes, halved
4 to 6 cups salad greens
2 to 3 cups julienned roasted turkey breast (page 36 or 37)
1/2 cup crumbled feta cheese
1/2 cup Greek olives

Whisk oil, lemon juice, mustard, oregano, marjoram, and garlic (if using) in a small bowl. Season with salt and pepper. Peel cucumber and cut into thick rounds. Cut each round into quarters. Combine cucumber, avocado, and tomatoes in a medium bowl. Toss with 2 to 3 tablespoons of the dressing.

Arrange salad greens on 4 to 6 plates. Divide cucumber mixture over greens. Arrange turkey over salads and sprinkle with feta and olives. Serve remaining dressing on the side.

Serves 4–6

HOLIDAY TURKEY & PAN GRAVY

1 (about 12lb) turkey, thawed if frozen
salt and freshly ground pepper, to taste
Oyster-Cornbread Stuffing (see page 40)
1 cup white wine or broth
4 cups turkey or chicken broth
1/3 cup cornstarch mixed with 1/2 cup cold water

Preheat oven to 350F (180C). Remove neck and giblets. Rinse turkey and pat dry. Season inside and out with salt and pepper. Place breast side up, in a V-shaped rack in a roasting pan. Loosely fill cavity with some stuffing; close opening with small skewers.

Roast turkey about 3 hours, until a thermometer inserted into the thickest part of thigh registers 180F (80C) and a thermometer inserted in the thickest part of breast registers 170F (75C). (Turkey needs about 15 minutes of cooking time per pound if stuffed.) The temperature of the center of the stuffing should be 160F (70C).

Remove turkey to a platter and cover with foil. Skim fat from pan juices; place pan over high heat. Stir in wine, stirring to loosen browned bits. Stir in broth and cornstarch mixture. Cook, stirring, until bubbly and thickened. Season with salt and pepper.

Serves 10–12

VARIATION: If you cooked the giblets for broth, chop them and add to the gravy.

OYSTER-CORNBREAD STUFFING

6 cups crumbled cornbread (see Note below)
4 cups dried bread cubes, part whole-grain
2 tablespoons minced fresh sage, or $2^{1}/_{2}$ teaspoons
   dried
2 tablespoons fresh thyme, or $2^{1}/_{2}$ teaspoons dried
2 teaspoons dried basil
8 tablespoons butter or margarine
1 large onion, chopped
4 celery stalks, chopped
2 ($^{1}/_{2}$-pint) jars fresh oysters
$3^{1}/_{2}$ cups turkey or chicken broth
salt and freshly ground pepper, to taste

Combine cornbread, bread cubes, and herbs in a large bowl; set aside.

Melt 6 tablespoons of the butter in a large skillet over medium heat. Add onion and celery and cook until softened. Add to bread mixture. Drain oysters, reserving liqueur; check for shell pieces. Add remaining 2 tablespoons butter to same skillet over medium heat. Add oysters; sauté until edges curl. Add reserved liqueur; bring to a boil. Add cooking juices to bread mixture. Cool oysters; chop with kitchen shears. Add to bread mixture. Stir in enough broth to make a very moist but not soupy mixture.

Use part of the stuffing to stuff the turkey or bake all in a casserole. Place remaining stuffing in a casserole, cover and refrigerate. Preheat oven to 350F (180C). Bake covered until hot, about 30 minutes.

Serves 12

NOTE: Cornbread can be made using your favorite recipe or a mix.

—— PERFECT ROAST CHICKEN ——

1 (6 to 8lb) roasting chicken
zest of 1 lemon
2 tablespoons minced fresh thyme, or 1 tablespoon
  dried
2 cloves garlic, minced
4 bay leaves
salt and freshly ground pepper, to taste
1$^{1}/_{2}$ cups white wine
1 cup half-and-half or light cream
1 tablespoon minced fresh flat-leaf parsley
1 tablespoon snipped fresh chives

Preheat oven to 425F (220C).

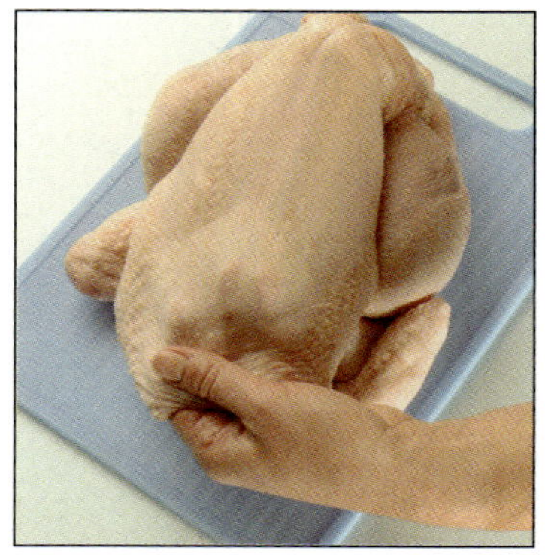

Remove giblets and reserve for other use.
Discard excess fat. Rinse chicken and pat
dry. Starting at the neck area, gently insert
your fingers under the skin to loosen, and
make a pocket. Combine lemon zest, thyme,
and garlic. Spread zest mixture under the
loosened breast skin. Place bay leaves under
skin. Season chicken with salt and pepper.
Place chicken in a V-shaped roasting rack
in a heavy roasting pan.

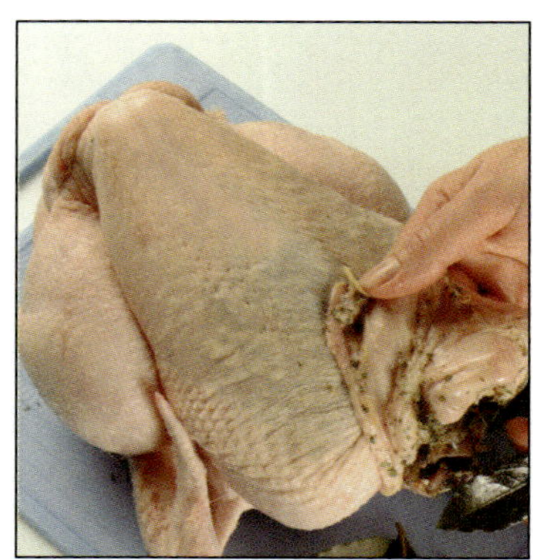

Roast about 1$^{1}/_{2}$ hours, until a thermometer
inserted into thickest part of thigh registers
180F (80C). Remove chicken to a platter;
let rest 10 minutes. Skim fat from pan
juices. Place pan over high heat; stir in
wine, stirring to loosen browned bits. Boil
until wine is reduced by half. Stir in half-
and-half, season with salt and pepper, and
heat until hot. Stir in parsley and chives.

Serves 6–8

ASIAN CHICKEN LEGS

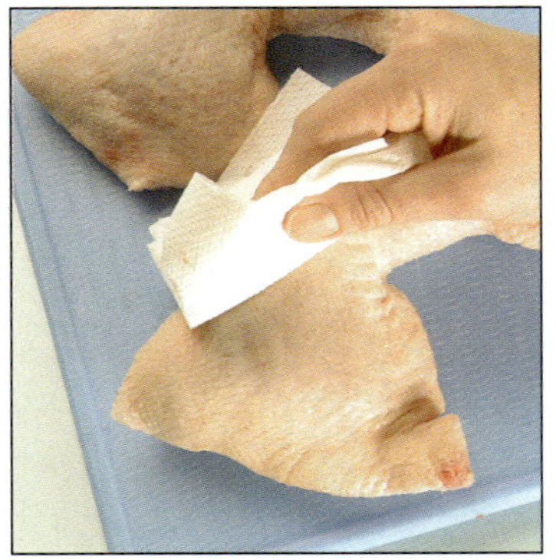

6 whole chicken legs
salt and freshly ground pepper, to taste
1/4 cup frozen apple juice concentrate, thawed
2 to 3 teaspoons five-spice powder

Preheat oven to 450F (230C). Rinse chicken and pat dry with paper towels. Season chicken with salt and pepper. Arrange chicken in a greased large heavy roasting pan. Roast 15 minutes.

Combine apple juice concentrate and five-spice powder in a small bowl.

Brush chicken with juice concentrate mixture. Roast about 10 minutes. Turn, brush with glaze, and roast about 10 minutes, until chicken is browned and juices run clear when chicken is pierced with a sharp knife.

Serves 6

CHICKEN WITH MARSALA SAUCE

6 boneless, skinless chicken breast halves
2 tablespoons olive oil
salt and freshly ground pepper, to taste
1/2 cup Marsala
1/2 cup chicken stock
1 tablespoon lemon juice
2 tablespoons capers
2 tablespoons butter, cut into 4 pieces

Preheat oven to 500F (260C). Pound chicken breasts with a mallet until flattened to about 1/2-inch thickness. Brush with olive oil and season with salt and pepper.

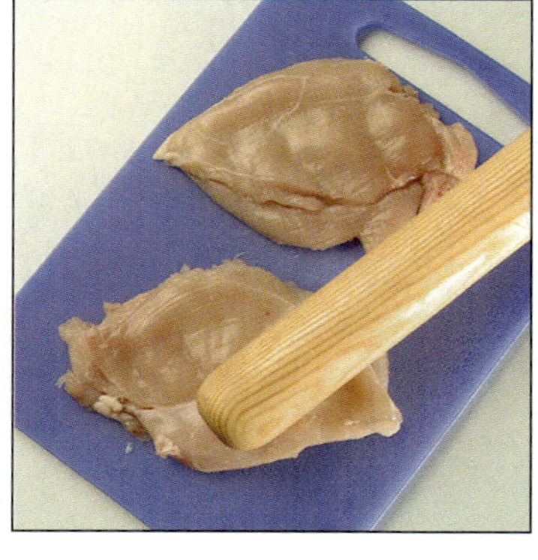

Place in a greased large and heavy roasting pan. Roast about 10 minutes, until cooked through. Remove chicken breasts to a platter; cover to keep warm.

Stir in Marsala to loosen browned bits; transfer to a saucepan. Add stock and boil over medium-high heat until reduced by half. Add lemon juice and capers. Season with salt and pepper. Reduce heat to low; add butter, one piece, at a time. Pour over chicken and serve.

Serves 6

—— SWEET & SPICY WINGS ——

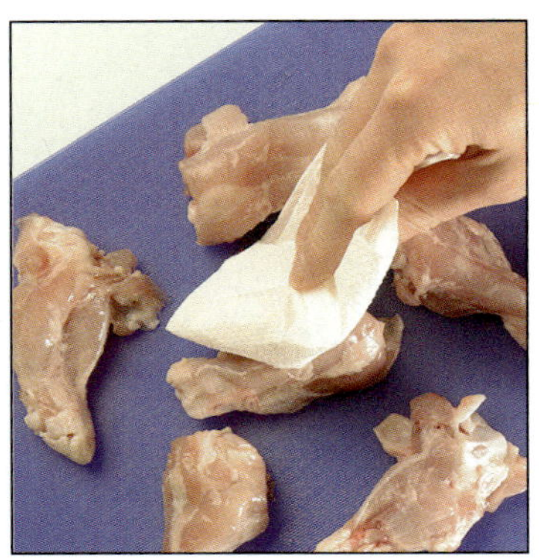

3lb chicken wings (see Note below)
$^1/_2$ cup apple jelly
2 teaspoons hot pepper sauce, or to taste (see Note below)
1 tablespoon Worcestershire sauce
1 tablespoon soy sauce
1 tablespoon olive oil
1 tablespoon white wine vinegar

Preheat oven to 450F (230C). Rinse wings with cold water and pat dry. Cut each wing into three pieces, cutting through the joints. Save wing tips for stock or discard. Place remaining pieces in a large bowl.

Melt apple jelly in a small saucepan over medium heat; remove from heat. Add remaining ingredients and stir to combine. Let cool. Pour jelly mixture over chicken wings and toss to combine. Stand for 10 minutes.

Transfer wings to a greased heavy roasting pan, reserving jelly mixture. Roast about 10 minutes. Turn and brush with jelly mixture; roast about 5 minutes, until cooked through.

Makes about 16 pieces

NOTE: Some markets sell "drumettes", the meaty parts of the wings. Purchase 2$^1/_2$lb, if available. The apple jelly mellows the hot pepper sauce; taste the jelly mixture before adding it to the chicken to get just the exact amount of heat required.

TANDOORI CHICKEN

1 (about 3lb) chicken, cut into serving pieces
1 lemon, halved
1/2 cup plain yogurt
1 tablespoon sweet paprika
2 teaspoons ground cumin
1/2 teaspoon salt
2 tablespoons finely minced ginger
2 large cloves garlic, finely minced
2 tablespoons olive oil

Rinse chicken and pat dry. Remove as much chicken skin as possible. Make 2 to 3 diagonal slashes in each chicken piece. Squeeze lemon over chicken.

Combine yogurt and remaining ingredients, except olive oil, in a large resealable plastic bag. Add chicken and coat with yogurt mixture. Refrigerate at least 3 hours or overnight.

Preheat oven to 400F (205C). Remove chicken and wipe off the yogurt mixture. Brush with olive oil. Arrange chicken on a rack in a large heavy roasting pan. Roast 25 minutes. Turn and roast about 20 minutes, until chicken is browned and juices are clear when chicken is pierced with a knife.

Serves 4–6

— CHICKEN & SWEET POTATO —

1 large sweet potato
2 tablespoons olive oil
1 (about 3lb) chicken, quartered
5 tablespoons Spicy Cajun Rub (page 88)
chopped fresh parsley, for garnish

Preheat oven to 425F (220C). Cut potato lengthwise into about 6 wedges, depending on size. Cut wedges crosswise if desired. Drizzle potato wedges with oil and rub to coat; sprinkle with 1 tablespoon of the rub. Place potato wedges in a heavy roasting pan.

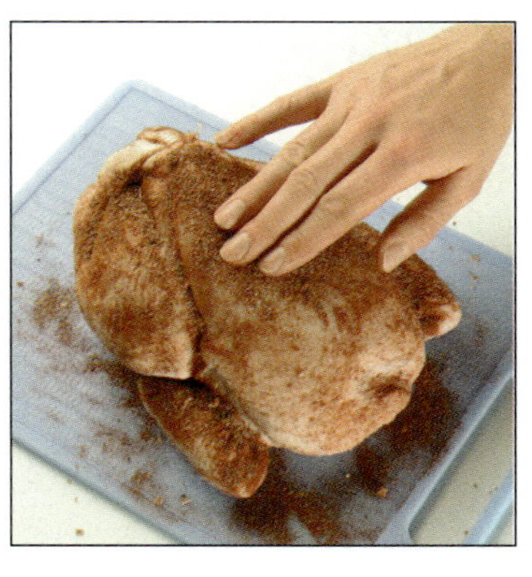

Rinse chicken and pat dry. Sprinkle chicken on all sides with remaining 4 tablespoons of rub; using your fingers, rub it in lightly, coating the chicken evenly. Place chicken on a rack over the potato in the roasting pan.

Roast for about 50 minutes, until a thermometer inserted through thickest part of thigh reads 180F (80C) and a thermometer inserted in thickest part of breast reads 170F (75C). (The breast pieces may need to be removed first.) Remove chicken and potato to a platter. Sprinkle parsley over potato wedges.

Serves 4

- CITRUS-MARINATED CHICKEN -

6 chicken breast halves with bones, skin removed
1 cup dried bread crumbs
salt and freshly ground pepper, to taste
orange wedges and mint sprigs, for garnish
GARLIC-CITRUS MARINADE:
1/4 cup olive oil
1/4 cup orange juice
1 tablespoon grated orange zest
2 tablespoons lemon juice
3 garlic cloves, minced
1 small onion, thinly sliced
2 teaspoons dried thyme

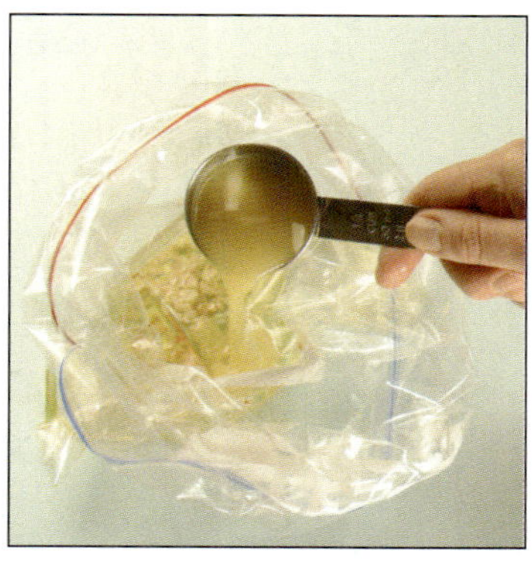

Combine marinade ingredients in a large resealable plastic bag.

Add chicken and turn to coat. Seal bag; refrigerate 2 hours or overnight. Preheat oven to 450F (230C). Remove chicken from marinade; discard marinade. Place crumbs, salt and pepper in a plastic bag. Add chicken; shake to coat.

Arrange chicken on a rack in a roasting pan. Roast about 20 minutes, until crumbs are browned and chicken is cooked through. Transfer to a serving plate; garnish with orange wedges and mint.

Serves 6

— CHICKEN & FRUIT SALAD —

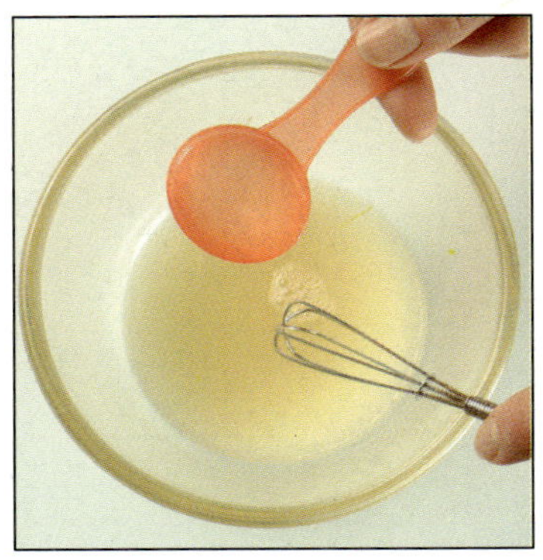

¹/4 cup frozen pineapple juice concentrate, thawed
2 tablespoons plain rice vinegar
1 tablespoon olive or canola oil
salt and freshly ground pepper, to taste
2 cups diced roasted chicken (page 41)
2 cups diced unpeeled apples tossed with 1
  tablespoon lemon juice
1 cup seedless red grapes, halved
¹/2 cup diced carrots
4 to 6 cups salad greens
¹/4 cup slivered almonds, toasted

Whisk together pineapple juice, vinegar, and oil in a small bowl. Season.

Add chicken, apples, grapes, and carrots to a large bowl. Toss with about 2 tablespoons of the dressing.

Arrange salad greens on 4 plates. Divide chicken mixture over greens. Garnish with almonds. Serve remaining dressing on the side.

Serves 4

— APRICOT-GLAZED QUAIL —

4 tablespoons butter
$1/2$ cup finely chopped celery
$1/4$ finely chopped onion
1 cup cooked white basmati rice, cooled
$1/4$ cup minced dried apricots
1 teaspoon ground sage
salt and freshly ground pepper
2 tablespoons olive oil
8 (about 4oz) quail, partially deboned
$1/2$ cup apricot jelly, melted with 1 tablespoon
   balsamic vinegar

Preheat oven to 350F (180C).

Melt butter in a skillet over medium heat. Add celery and onion and sauté until softened. Stir in rice, apricots, and sage. Season with salt and pepper. Set aside to cool. Rinse quail and pat dry with paper towels. Stuff each quail with about $1/8$ of the stuffing. Heat oil in a large skillet over medium-high heat. Add quail, breast sides down, in batches and cook until browned. Transfer quail to roasting pan, breast sides up.

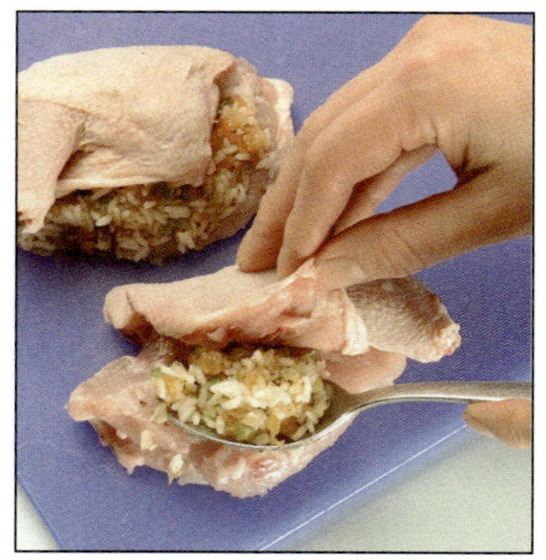

Brush quail with apricot jelly. Roast about 15 minutes, until juices run clear and thighs are tender. Do not overcook.

Serves 4

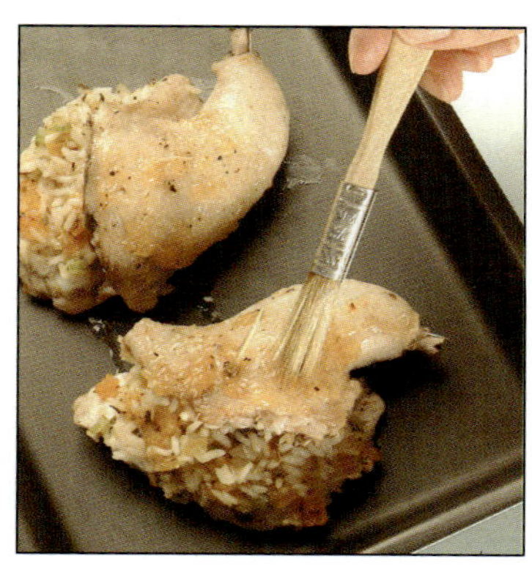

— HOISIN-GLAZED GAME HENS —

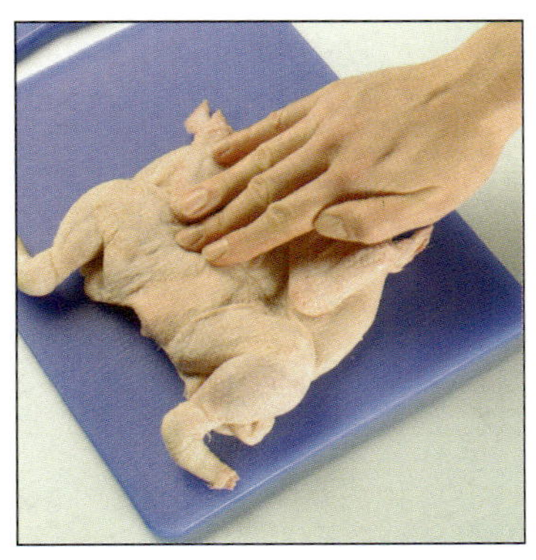

2 (about 1^3/4lb) Cornish game hens or poussins
1^1/2 tablespoons sesame oil
salt and freshly ground pepper, to taste
^{1}/4 cup mango chutney
^{1}/4 cup hoisin sauce
2 zucchini, cut diagonally into ^{3}/4-inch slices

Preheat oven to 450F (230C). Rinse hens with cold water and pat dry. Cut hens along the backbone and flatten by pressing down on the breastbone with your hand. (Cut out and discard backbones if desired.)

Arrange hens on a rack in a roasting pan in the middle of the oven. Brush with 1 tablespoon of the sesame oil and season with salt and pepper. Roast for about 10 minutes. Meanwhile, finely mince large pieces of fruit in chutney; combine chutney and hoisin sauce in a small bowl.

Brush hens with sauce mixture. Add zucchini to rack next to game hens and brush with remaining sesame oil. Roast 10 minutes. Turn and brush with sauce mixture. Roast hens about 15 minutes or until cooked through and the thigh juices run clear when pierced with a knife, a thermometer inserted into thigh registers 180F (80C), and zucchini are crisp-tender.

Serves 4

CRISPY DUCK WITH TAMARIND

1 (about 5lb) duck, thawed if frozen
1 lemon, quartered
salt and freshly ground pepper, to taste
1 cup tamarind concentrate (see Note below)
6 tablespoons mild honey, such as clover or orange
  blossom
1 tablespoon cornstarch mixed with 1/2 cup chicken
  broth

Preheat oven to 400F (205C). Rinse duck and trim off excess fat with kitchen shears. Prick duck all over with a sharp fork. Season inside and out with salt and pepper. Place lemon quarters in duck cavity.

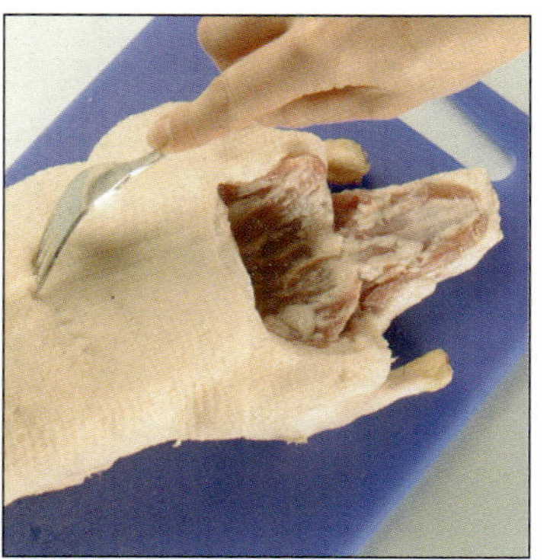

Place duck, breast side up, in a V-shaped rack in a roasting pan. Roast duck about 1 hour; remove fat with a bulb baster every 30 minutes. Meanwhile, heat tamarind concentrate and honey in a saucepan over medium heat until honey melts. Begin basting duck with 1/3 cup of the tamarind mixture; reserve remainder for serving. Baste 2 to 3 times on all sides; roast 30 to 40 minutes, until a thermometer inserted into thigh registers 180F (80C), juices run clear, and drumsticks move freely. (Duck needs 15 to 20 minutes of cooking time per pound.)

Transfer duck to a cutting board. Stand for 10 minutes. Cut duck into pieces. Combine remaining tamarind mixture with cornstarch mixture in a saucepan; cook over medium heat until bubbly and slightly thickened; serve on the side.

Serves 2–4

NOTE: If only tamarind paste is available, boil 1 tablespoon with 1 cup water or chicken broth in a small saucepan. Strain out seeds and strings.

DUCK & POMEGRANATE SAUCE

¹/₂ cup pomegranate molasses (see Note below)
¹/₃ cup orange juice
1 tablespoon seasoned rice vinegar
1 tablespoon grated orange zest
4 (4 to 6oz) duck breasts
salt and freshly ground pepper, to taste
about ¹/₂ cup fresh pomegranate seeds
segments of 1 orange

Preheat oven to 500F (260C). Heat pomegranate molasses, orange juice, vinegar, and orange zest in a small saucepan over medium heat until hot; set aside.

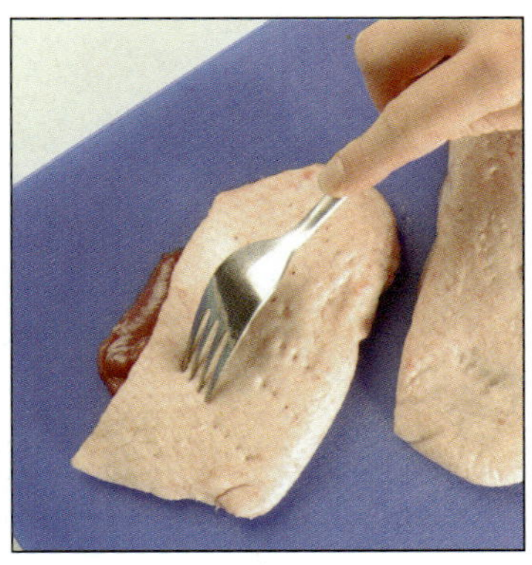

Prick duck skin with a sharp fork. Season with salt and pepper. Place duck on a rack in a heavy roasting pan. Roast about 10 minutes for medium rare, or to desired doneness. If skin is not crisp, brush with a little sauce and broil 2 to 3 minutes, until browned and crispy.

Spoon pools of sauce on dinner plates; place duck breasts on sauce. Sprinkle with pomegranate seeds and garnish with orange segments.

Serves 4

NOTE: Pomegranate molasses are available at stores that sell Middle Eastern foods. Red currant jelly could be used instead, but the flavor will be different.

GOOSE WITH WINE PAN SAUCE

1 (about 10lb) young goose, thawed if frozen
1 small onion, quartered
1 orange, quartered
1 stalk celery, cut into 4 pieces
salt and freshly ground pepper, to taste
1/2 cup each chopped onion, celery, and carrot
1 cup white wine
2 cups chicken broth
2 tablespoons cornstarch mixed with 1/2 cup orange
  juice

Preheat oven to 400F (205C). Rinse goose and trim excess fat with kitchen shears.

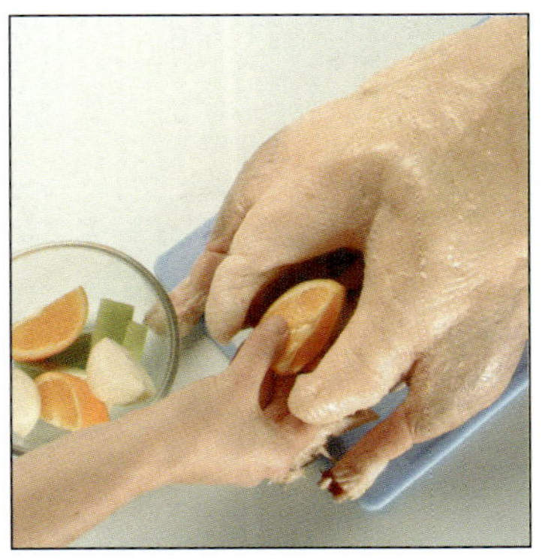

Prick goose all over with a sharp fork. Place onion quarters, orange, and celery stalk in goose cavity. Season inside and out with salt and pepper. Place goose, breast side up, in a V-shaped rack in a large heavy roasting pan. Add about 1 inch of water to bottom of pan (this prevents you from having to remove the fat until the end of roasting time). Roast goose about 2 hours, until a thermometer inserted into thickest part of thigh registers 180F (80C), juices run clear, and drumsticks move freely. (The goose needs 10 to 15 minutes of cooking time per pound.)

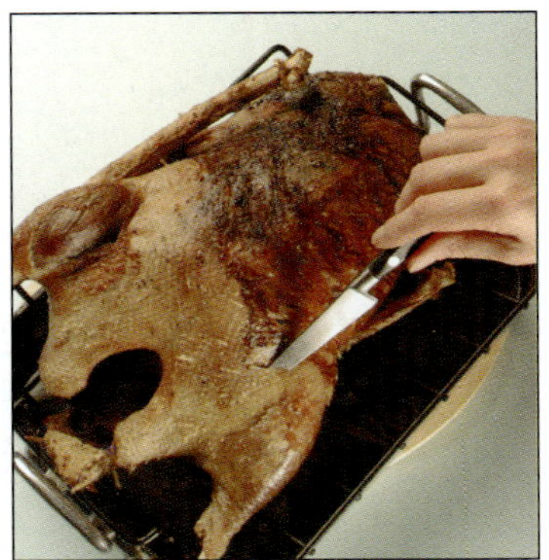

Remove goose to a platter; cover with foil. Skim fat from pan juices, place pan over high heat, and stir in chopped onion, celery, and carrots. Cook, stirring, until vegetables are softened. Add wine, and cook, stirring to loosen browned bits and vegetables. Stir in broth and cornstarch mixture. Cook, stirring, until bubbly and thickened. Season with salt and pepper.

Serves 6–8

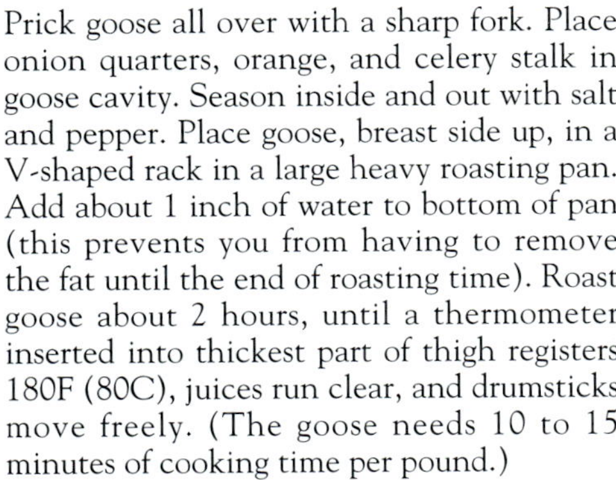

— BASIL-ENCRUSTED HALIBUT —

4 (6oz) halibut fillets (about 1 inch thick)
8 tablespoons pesto
salt and freshly ground pepper, to taste
1/2 cup fine fresh bread crumbs
1 large clove garlic, minced
2 tablespoons pine nuts, toasted

Preheat oven to 450F (230C). Spray a heavy baking sheet with cooking spray. Spread fillets with pesto; season with salt and pepper. Arrange fillets on baking sheet.

Combine crumbs and garlic in a small bowl. Divide crumb mixture among fillets; press to adhere.

Roast fillets 10 to 15 minutes, just until fish begins to flake. Sprinkle with toasted pine nuts.

Serves 4

COD WITH VEGETABLES

2 carrots, peeled
1 small red bell pepper
1 medium leek
1^1/$_2$ tablespoons olive oil
1 tablespoon water
salt and freshly ground pepper, to taste
4 (6oz) cod fillets (about 1 inch thick)
1 tablespoon chopped fresh dill, or 1 teaspoon dried

Preheat oven to 450F (230C). Cut carrots crosswise, and into 1/4-inch strips. Cut bell pepper into half crosswise. Remove core and seeds. Cut lengthwise into 1/4-inch strips.

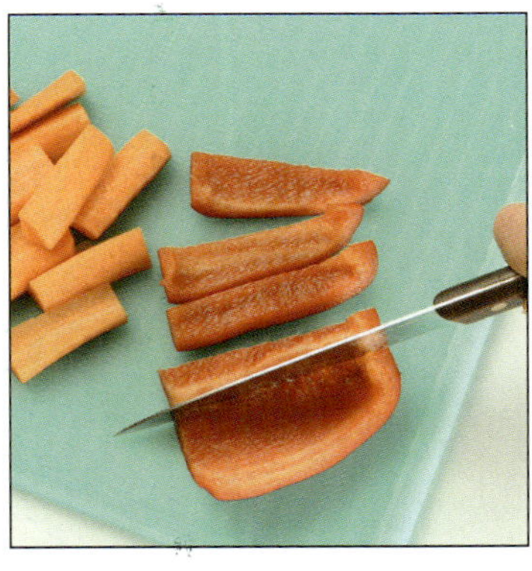

Cut off green leek top. Slit white part along one side and rinse well under running water to remove any dirt and grit. Cut leek into thin strips. Combine vegetables in a large bowl. Add 1 tablespoon of the oil, water, salt, and pepper; toss to combine.

Arrange cod in a greased roasting pan. Drizzle with remaining oil. Season with dill, salt, and pepper. Arrange vegetables around cod. Roast 10 to 15 minutes, just until fish begins to flake and vegetables are crisp-tender.

Serves 4

SALAD NIÇOISE

4 small yellow-fleshed potatoes, quartered
about 6 tablespoons extra-virgin olive oil
salt and freshly ground pepper, to taste
1lb ahi tuna steak (about 1 inch thick)
4 tablespoons fresh lemon juice
1 tablespoon Dijon mustard
4 to 6 cups salad greens
2 cups cherry tomatoes, halved
1/4 cup Niçoise olives

Preheat oven to 425F (220C). Toss potatoes with 1 tablespoon of olive oil, salt, and pepper. Transfer to a heavy roasting pan.

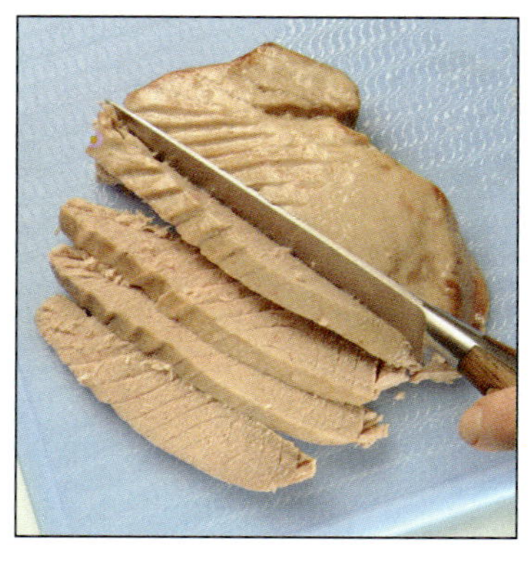

Roast potatoes about 25 minutes, until tender. Brush tuna with a little olive oil; season with salt and pepper. Place on a roasting rack and roast about 10 minutes, until outside is white and center is still pink. Cut tuna into thin slices.

Combine remaining 4 tablespoons olive oil, lemon juice, and mustard in a small bowl. Arrange salad greens on 4 large serving plates. Arrange tuna, potatoes, green beans, tomatoes, and olives over greens. Drizzle with dressing.

Serves 4

— GROUPER WITH RIPE OLIVES —

4 (6oz) grouper fillets (about 1 inch thick)
1^1/$_2$ tablespoons olive oil
salt and freshly ground pepper, to taste
2 medium tomatoes
1 large clove garlic, minced
1 teaspoon dried oregano
^{1}/$_2$ cup Greek olives

Preheat oven to 450F (230C). Spray a heavy baking sheet with cooking spray. Place fillets on baking sheet. Brush with 1 tablespoon of the olive oil. Season with salt and pepper.

Cut an "X" in the blossom end of each tomato. Place in boiling water for about 30 seconds. Transfer to ice water to cool. Peel tomatoes; cut in half crosswise. Squeeze to remove most of the seeds and juice. Coarsely chop.

Combine tomatoes, garlic, oregano, olives, and remaining olive oil in a bowl. Spoon around the fillets. Roast 10 to 12 minutes, until fish just begins to flake.

Serves 4

– SNAPPER WITH CITRUS SAUCE –

4 (4 to 6oz) snapper fillets
1 teaspoon minced fresh tarragon or $^1/_2$ teaspoon
  dried
sweet paprika, for dusting (optional)
salt and freshly ground pepper, to taste
1 red or pink grapefruit
2 tablespoons butter

Preheat oven to 450F (230C). Spray a heavy baking sheet with cooking spray. Arrange fillets in a single layer on a heavy baking sheet. Sprinkle fillets with tarragon and paprika (if using). Season with salt and pepper.

Peel grapefruit and cut into segments, working over a bowl to catch the juice. Arrange segments around fillets. Squeeze juice from membranes into the bowl and pour over the fillets. Roast about 8 minutes, until fish just begins to flake. Transfer fillets and grapefruit to a serving platter.

Pour juices from baking sheet into a small saucepan over medium heat. Add butter, one piece at a time; stir until melted. Pour sauce over fillets and grapefruit.

Serves 4

CRAB-STUFFED TROUT

4 (10 to 12oz) trout, ready to cook
salt and freshly ground pepper, to taste
1/4 cup finely chopped celery
1 tablespoon minced shallot
1 tablespoon butter
3/4 cup fresh bread crumbs
1/4 cup mayonnaise
1 teaspoon Dijon mustard
1 egg, beaten
dash hot pepper sauce
1/2lb crabmeat

Preheat oven to 450F (230C).

Rinse trout and pat dry. Arrange trout on a greased large baking sheet. Season inside and out with salt and pepper. Set aside. Cook celery and shallot in butter over medium heat until softened. Combine bread crumbs, celery mixture, mayonnaise, mustard, egg, and hot pepper sauce in a bowl. Gently stir in crabmeat. Divide mixture into 4 portions.

Stuff each trout with crab mixture. Roast about 20 minutes, until trout just begins to flake and a thermometer inserted in the stuffing reads 160F (70C).

Serves 4

— FISH ROLLS WITH TAPENADE —

4 (6oz) fish fillets, such as snapper
4 tablespoons tapenade
olive oil
freshly ground pepper, to taste
1 cup Rustic Tomato Sauce (page 86)

Preheat oven to 450F (230C). Lay fillets out on a work surface. Spread each fillet with 1 tablespoon of the tapenade.

Roll up each fillet like a jelly roll. Fasten ends with wooden picks. Place rolls in a greased roasting pan. Brush lightly with olive oil; season with pepper.

Spoon tomato sauce around fillets. Roast about 10 minutes, until fish just begins to flake. Remove wooden picks before serving.

Serves 4

— VEGETABLE-STUFFED SALMON —

2 (1lb) salmon fillets with skin
salt and freshly ground pepper
VEGETABLE STUFFING:
2 tablespoons butter or margarine
1/2 cup finely chopped celery
1/4 cup finely chopped onion
1/4 cup finely chopped red bell pepper
1/4 cup minced flat-leaf parsley
1 tablespoon minced fresh tarragon
salt and freshly ground pepper
lemon slices, for garnish
fresh tarragon and parsley sprigs, for garnish

Preheat oven to 400F (205C).

Rinse fillets and pat dry. Season with salt
and pepper. To make sauce, melt butter in a
large skillet over medium heat. Add celery,
onion, and bell pepper; sauté until tender.
Add remaining ingredients except
garnishes; stir to combine. Season with salt
and pepper. Place one fillet, skin side down,
on a work surface. Top with stuffing. Place
remaining fillet, skin side up, over stuffing.
Tie with kitchen twine to close edges.

Place in a greased heavy roasting pan. Roast
about 10 minutes per 2cm (1 inch), or until
fish is 140F (60C) and begins to flake.
Transfer to a serving platter and remove
twine and upper skin. Garnish with lemon
slices and herb sprigs.

Serves 4–6

SPICY CRAB CAKES

$^1/4$ cup chopped celery
2 tablespoons minced shallots
1 tablespoon minced jalapeño chile
1 tablespoon butter
$^3/4$ cup fresh bread crumbs, made from home-made style bread
$^1/4$ cup mayonnaise
1 teaspoon Dijon mustard
1 egg, beaten
$^1/8$ teaspoon cayenne pepper, or to taste
12oz crabmeat

Preheat oven to 450F (230C). Cook celery, shallots, and chile in butter until softened.

Spray a heavy baking sheet with cooking spray. Combine bread crumbs, celery mixture, mayonnaise, mustard, egg, and cayenne in a bowl. Gently stir in crabmeat. Divide mixture into 8 portions.

Shape each portion into a slightly rounded patty. Place on prepared baking sheet. Roast in bottom third of oven for 5 minutes. Turn and roast about 5 minutes, until browned.

Makes 8 crab cakes

SCALLOPS & TARRAGON SAUCE

1lb sea scallops
olive oil
salt and freshly ground pepper, to taste
TARRAGON SAUCE:
1 cup dry white wine
1 cup bottled clam juice
$^1\!/_2$ cup heavy cream
1 tablespoon chopped fresh tarragon or 1 teaspoon
  dried
1 tablespoon minced fresh chives
1 tablespoon sun-dried or regular tomato paste

Preheat oven to 500F (260C).

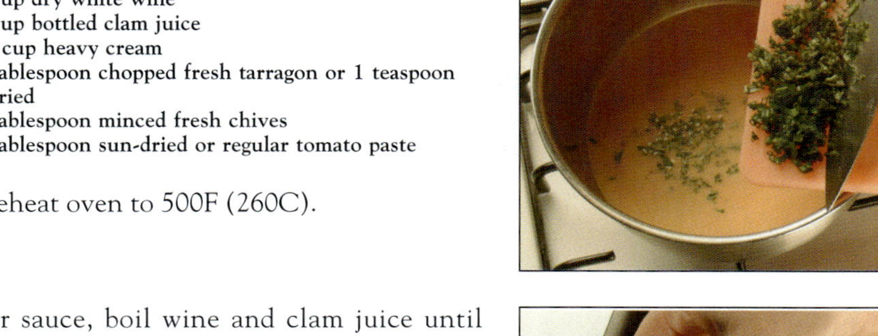

For sauce, boil wine and clam juice until reduced to about $^1\!/_2$ cup. Whisk in cream and tomato paste. Stir in tarragon and chives. Season with salt and pepper. Keep warm. Spray a non-stick roasting pan with cooking spray. Rinse scallops and pat dry with paper towels. Arrange scallops in prepared pan in a single layer.

Brush scallops with olive oil. Season with salt and pepper. Roast scallops 5 to 10 minutes, or until opaque and firm. Do not overcook. Serve scallops with sauce.

Serves 3–4

SPICY ROASTED SHRIMP

1lb uncooked medium shrimp
2 tablespoons olive oil
2 tablespoons crushed red pepper
2 garlic cloves, minced
$1/2$ teaspoon salt
1 teaspoon coarsely ground black pepper
2 tablespoons chopped fresh parsley
lemon wedges, to serve

Peel and devein shrimp, leaving tails on if desired.

Combine olive oil, crushed red pepper, garlic, salt, and pepper in a medium bowl. Add shrimp and toss to combine. Let stand while oven heats.

Preheat oven to 500F (260C). Transfer shrimp and seasoning to a large heavy roasting pan, arranging shrimp in a single layer. Roast about 5 minutes, until shrimp are pink, stirring once. Transfer shrimp to a serving dish. Sprinkle with parsley. Serve with lemon wedges.

Serves 4

OYSTERS & VINAIGRETTE

24 medium oysters in shells
TOMATO VINAIGRETTE:
¼ cup seasoned rice vinegar
2 tablespoons olive oil
1 teaspoon Dijon mustard
hot pepper sauce, to taste
1 cup minced fresh tomatoes

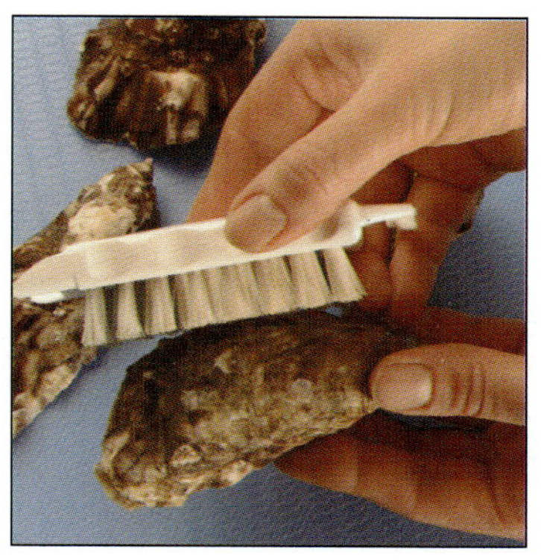

Preheat oven to 500F (260C). Scrub oysters with a stiff brush. Discard any oysters that remain open.

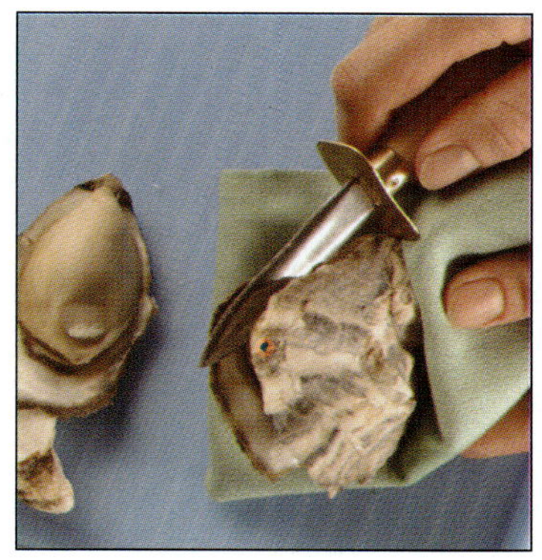

Arrange oysters in one layer on 2 heavy baking sheets. Roast about 10 minutes, until oysters open slightly. Open oysters with an oyster knife, protecting your hand with a heavy glove.

Whisk vinegar, oil, mustard and hot pepper sauce in a small bowl. Stir in tomatoes. Serve oysters on the half shell with sauce.

Serves 4

TOMATO & BASIL SOUP

3 1/2lb tomatoes
1 medium onion, cut into 1/2-inch-thick slices
2 large cloves garlic, peeled
2 tablespoons olive oil
2 tablespoons slivered basil, plus extra for topping
1 3/4 cups vegetable or chicken broth
1/2 cup whipping cream or crème fraiche
salt and freshly ground pepper, to taste
4 thin goat cheese rounds
4 teaspoons pesto (optional)

Preheat oven to 450F (230C). Cut tomatoes in half crosswise. Squeeze out some of the seeds and juice. Cut each half into quarters.

Combine onion, garlic, tomatoes, and olive oil in a large bowl. Toss to combine. Transfer mixture to a greased heavy roasting pan. Roast about 45 minutes, until most of the juices have evaporated and tomatoes just begin to brown on the edges. Roasting time will depend on the type of tomato and how much juice the tomatoes contain.

Transfer tomato mixture to a food mill or press through a strainer to remove seeds and peels. Transfer sieved mixture to a saucepan and stir in broth. Bring to a boil. Stir in cream and basil; season with salt and pepper. Ladle soup into bowls. Center a cheese round in each bowl; top with pesto (if using). Sprinkle with additional basil.

Serves 4

SPICED CAULIFLOWER

1 head cauliflower (2^1/$_2$ to 3lb)
2 tablespoons olive oil
2 tablespoons water
1 teaspoon ground paprika
^{1}/$_2$ teaspoon ground mace
^{1}/$_2$ teaspoon ground mustard
salt and freshly ground pepper, to taste
^{1}/$_4$ cup slivered almonds

Preheat oven to 500F (260C). Divide cauliflower into small florets.

Combine oil, water, paprika, mace, and mustard in a large bowl. Add cauliflower and toss to combine. Season with salt and pepper.

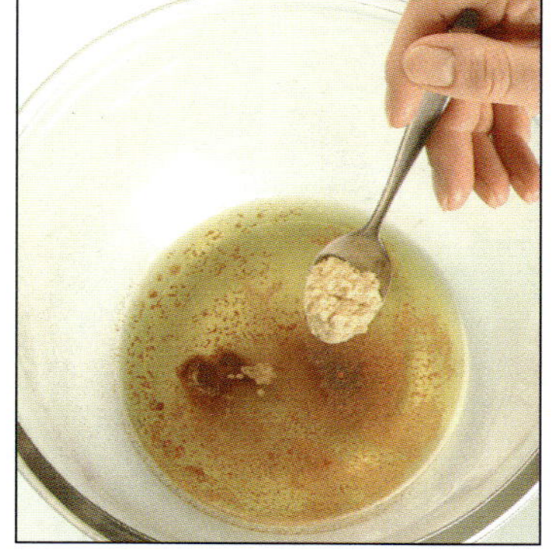

Transfer cauliflower to a large heavy roasting pan. Roast 10 minutes. Turn and add almonds. Roast 3 to 5 minutes, until almonds are toasted and cauliflower is crisp-tender.

Serves 4–6

SPICY PLANTAINS

4 very ripe (blackened) medium plantains
1 tablespoon butter, melted
1 tablespoon olive oil
1/4 cup fresh lime juice
salt, to taste
1 tablespoon grated lime zest
1 teaspoon red pepper flakes, or to taste (optional)

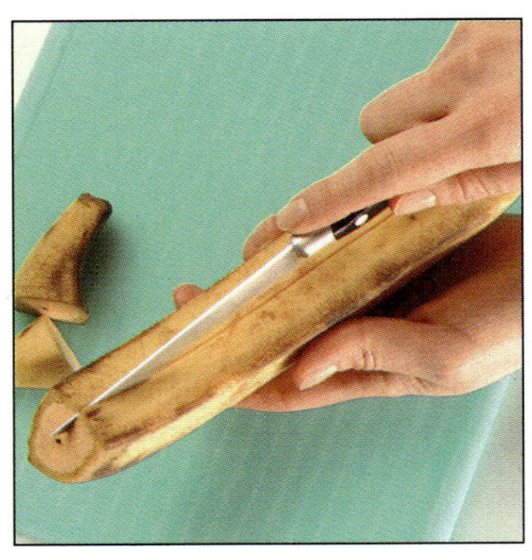

Preheat oven to 450F (230C). Cut ends off plantains and cut a lengthwise slit in the skin of each plantain to make peeling easier; peel.

Cut plantains crosswise into 1-inch pieces. Toss plantains, butter, oil, and lime juice in a medium bowl. Season with salt. Place plantains in heavy roasting pan. Roast in the middle of the oven for about 8 minutes. Turn and roast about 5 minutes, until tender when pierced with a fork.

Combine remaining ingredients and sprinkle over plantain slices. Serve hot.

Serves 4

BEETS WITH GINGER

4 medium beets
1 tablespoon canola oil plus extra for rubbing
2 tablespoons plain rice vinegar
2 teaspoons grated fresh ginger
1 teaspoon soy sauce
1/2 teaspoon sugar
1 tablespoon thinly sliced green onion

Preheat oven to 400F (205C). Remove beet tops, leaving a small amount of stems. Scrub beets and pat dry. Rub beets with a little oil. Place in a roasting pan. Roast about 1 hour, until beets are tender when pierced with a knife.

Combine vinegar, 1 tablespoon oil, ginger, soy sauce, and sugar in a medium bowl. Stir until sugar dissolves.

Let beets stand until cool enough to handle. Peel and cut into 1-inch pieces. Add warm beets to dressing. Toss to combine. Garnish with green onion.

Serves 4

VARIATION: Beets can be peeled and cubed before roasting to reduce the cooking time. Roast at 500F (260C) 10 to 15 minutes, turning once. Toss with dressing.

─ BABY CARROTS WITH HONEY ─

1 tablespoon butter
1 tablespoon canola oil
1 tablespoon honey
1 tablespoon lemon juice
$\frac{1}{2}$ teaspoon vanilla extract
1lb baby carrots, halved if large
salt, to taste
1 tablespoon grated lemon zest
2 tablespoons dried zante currants (optional)

Preheat oven to 450F (230C). Melt butter in a large skillet over medium heat. Add oil, honey, lemon juice, and vanilla. Heat until honey melts.

Add carrots, season with salt, and toss to combine. Transfer carrots to a large heavy roasting pan. Roast in middle of oven about 8 minutes. Stir and roast about 5 minutes, until carrots are crisp-tender.

Transfer carrots to a serving dish and sprinkle with lemon zest and currants (if using). Serve hot.

Serves 4

— LEEKS WITH GOATS CHEESE —

1lb small leeks (4 to 6 leeks)
2 tablespoons olive oil
2 tablespoons balsamic vinegar
salt and freshly ground pepper, to taste
2oz goat cheese or feta, crumbled
2 tablespoons snipped chives

Preheat oven to 450F (230C). Cut green tops and root ends off leeks. Cut leeks lengthwise almost to the centers. Rinse under cold running water to remove any sand and dirt.

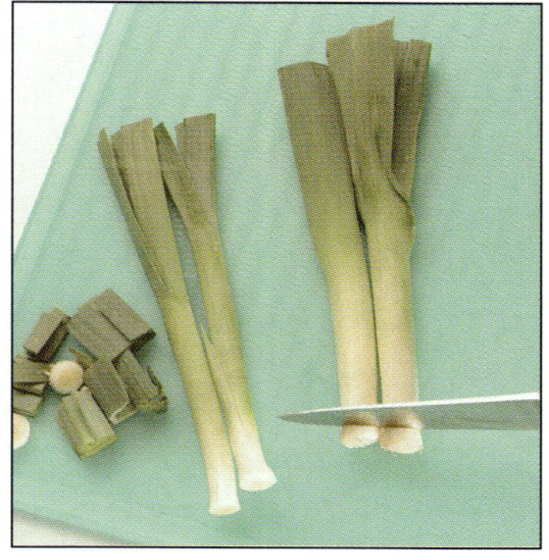

Place leeks in large heavy roasting pan. Drizzle each leek with oil and vinegar. Season with salt and pepper. Roast in middle of oven about 10 minutes. Turn and roast about 10 minutes, until leeks have softened.

Arrange leeks on a serving dish. Top with goat cheese and chives.

Serves 4

— ROSEMARY-POTATO WEDGES —

2lb long yellow-fleshed potatoes
1 tablespoon olive oil
1 tablespoon water
1 teaspoon rosemary
2 large cloves garlic, halved (optional)
salt and freshly ground pepper, to taste

Preheat oven to 450F (230C). Cut each potato lengthwise into 6 or 8 wedges, depending on size.

Place potatoes into a large bowl. Add olive oil, water, rosemary, and garlic (if using). Season with salt and pepper. Toss to combine.

Transfer potatoes to a large heavy roasting pan. Roast in the middle of the oven about 15 minutes. Turn and roast about 15 minutes, until potatoes are tender when pierced with a knife.

Serves 6

—— ROASTED POTATO SALAD ——

1lb red-skinned potatoes (about 6)
1 medium sweet onion
1 medium red bell pepper
1 medium green bell pepper
2 tablespoons olive oil
1 tablespoon water
salt and freshly ground pepper, to taste
2 tablespoons mayonnaise
2 tablespoons heavy cream or yogurt
1 tablespoon white wine vinegar
1 teaspoon Dijon mustard
1 tablespoon minced fresh dill or 1 teaspoon dried
1 teaspoon mustard seeds, toasted over medium heat
  until aromatic

Preheat oven to 450F (230C). Scrub potatoes. Cut unpeeled potatoes into 1-inch pieces. Peel onion and core bell peppers, and cut into 1-inch pieces. Place potatoes, onion, and bell peppers in a large bowl. Add olive oil and water. Season with salt and pepper and toss to combine. Transfer to a large heavy roasting pan. Roast 10 minutes. Stir and roast about 10 minutes, until vegetables are tender, but hold their shapes.

Whisk mayonnaise, cream, vinegar, mustard, minced or dried dill, and mustard seeds in a small bowl. Transfer vegetables to a bowl. Add dressing and toss to combine. Season with salt and pepper. Serve warm or chilled.

Serves 6

ROOTS WITH NUTMEG

1 rutabaga
1 turnip
2 parsnips
2 carrots
2 tablespoons olive oil
1 tablespoon water
$1/2$ teaspoon ground nutmeg, preferably freshly
  grated
salt and freshly ground pepper, to taste

Preheat oven to 500F (260C). Peel all vegetables and cut into thin 2-inch strips.

Place vegetables in a large bowl. Add oil, water, and nutmeg; season with salt and pepper. Toss to combine.

Transfer vegetables to a heavy roasting pan. Roast in the middle of the oven about 10 minutes. Stir and roast about 10 minutes, until vegetables are tender.

Serves 6

VEGETABLE MEDLEY

12oz globe eggplant
1 large red bell pepper
1 large tomato, chopped
6oz fresh mushrooms
$^{1}/_{2}$ cup chopped onion
1 large clove garlic, chopped
2 tablespoons olive oil
1 tablespoon white wine vinegar
1 teaspoon dried oregano
salt and freshly ground pepper, to taste

Preheat oven to 500F (260C). Peel eggplant and cut into 1-inch cubes.

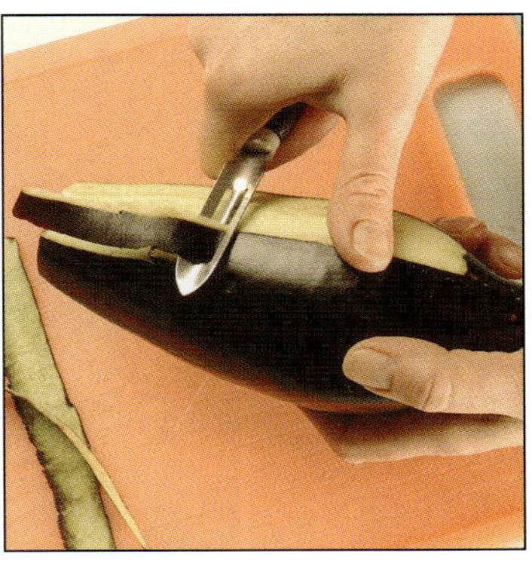

Core and seed bell pepper and cut into 1-inch squares. Coarsely chop tomato. Halve or quarter mushrooms if large. Combine vegetables, garlic, oil, vinegar, and oregano in a large bowl. Season with salt and pepper; toss to combine.

Transfer vegetables to a large heavy roasting pan. Roast about 8 minutes. Stir and roast 5 minutes, until vegetables are tender. Spoon into pita pockets, use as a dip, or as a salad.

Serves 4

— EGGPLANT & CHEESE STACKS —

1 (about 12oz) slender globe eggplant
salt
1 large red bell pepper
2 tablespoons olive oil
freshly ground pepper, to taste
$^1/_4$ cup pesto
$^3/_4$ cup shredded provolone or mozzarella cheese
6 tomato slices
2 teaspoons dried oregano
$^1/_2$ cup freshly grated parmesan cheese

Preheat oven to 500F (260C). Cut eggplant crosswise into 1-inch slices. Salt eggplant slices.

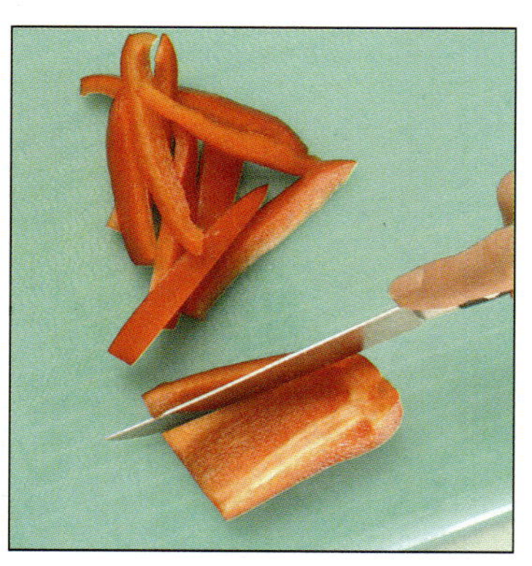

Let eggplant stand in a strainer about 30 minutes. Rinse and pat dry. Core and seed bell pepper and cut into thin strips. Brush eggplant and bell pepper with olive oil. Season with salt and pepper. Arrange in a greased heavy roasting pan. Roast about 10 minutes, until tender, turning once. Leave oven on.

Spread each eggplant slice with pesto. Top with a tomato slice, then with about 1 tablespoon provolone. Sprinkle with oregano. Arrange bell pepper strips over each stack; sprinkle with parmesan. Return to the oven until cheese melts. Serve as an appetizer or vegetarian sandwich filling.

Serves 4–6

BABY ARTICHOKES WITH LEMON

12 baby artichokes (about 2oz each)
3 tablespoons olive oil
2 tablespoons dry white wine
1 tablespoon chopped fresh thyme or 1 teaspoon
  dried
salt and freshly ground pepper
thyme sprigs, for garnish
lemon wedges, to serve

Preheat oven to 400F (205C). Break off outer dark artichoke leaves. Cut about 1 inch off tops. Peel stems.

Cut artichokes in half lengthwise. Rinse, drain well, and pat dry with paper towels.

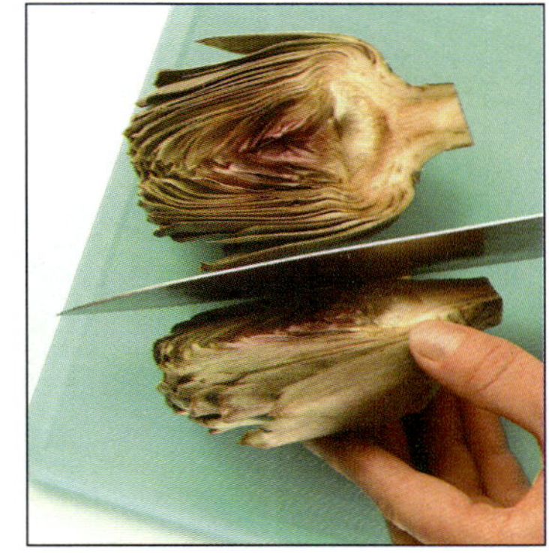

Arrange artichokes in a large heavy roasting pan. Drizzle with oil and wine and sprinkle with thyme, salt, and pepper. Cover with foil and roast 45 minutes to 1 hour, until tender. Transfer to a serving dish. Garnish with thyme sprigs and serve with lemon wedges.

Serves 4

- ASPARAGUS, ORANGE, & MINT -

1lb fresh green asparagus
2 tablespoons olive oil
salt and freshly ground pepper
1/4 cup fresh orange juice
1 tablespoon grated orange zest
1 tablespoon minced fresh mint
fresh mint sprigs, for garnish

Preheat oven to 500F (260C). Break tough ends off asparagus.

Arrange asparagus in a single layer in a large heavy roasting pan. Drizzle with oil and turn to coat. Roast in center of oven 5 minutes. Turn and roast about 5 minutes more depending on size of spears, until crisp-tender.

Transfer to a serving dish. Season with salt and pepper, and toss with orange juice. Transfer to a serving dish. Sprinkle with orange zest and mint; garnish with mint sprigs. Serve warm.

Serves 2–4

── BROCCOLI & BLUE CHEESE ──

1 to 2 tablespoons olive oil
1 tablespoon water
salt and freshly ground black pepper, to taste
$1/8$ teaspoon cayenne pepper, or to taste (optional)
4 cups fresh broccoli florets (about 10oz)
$1/4$ cup crumbled blue cheese

Preheat oven to 425F (220C). Whisk together oil, water, salt, black pepper, and cayenne, if using, in a large bowl. Add broccoli and toss to coat.

Arrange broccoli in one layer in a large heavy roasting pan. Roast about 10 minutes, turning once, until edges are browned and broccoli is crisp-tender.

Transfer broccoli to a serving bowl and immediately toss with cheese.

Serves 2–4

— BRUSSEL SPROUTS & POTATO —

1lb sweet potato
8oz fresh Brussels sprouts
2 tablespoons olive oil
1 tablespoon water
salt and freshly ground pepper to taste

Preheat oven to 500F (260C). Peel sweet potato and cut crosswise into 3/4-inch slices. Cut slices into quarters.

Trim Brussels sprouts and cut lengthwise into halves. In a bowl toss sweet potato and Brussels sprouts with remaining ingredients. Arrange in one layer in a large heavy roasting pan.

Roast about 10 minutes; turn. Roast 5 minutes more, until tender. Serve hot.

Serves 4

GREEN BEANS WITH WALNUTS

1lb fresh green beans
1 tablespoon olive oil
1 tablespoon water
1 tablespoon fresh savory or 1 teaspoon dried
salt and freshly ground pepper, to taste
$^1/_3$ cup chopped walnut halves, roasted (see below)

Preheat oven to 500F (260C). Remove ends from beans and remove any strings.

Whisk together oil, water, savory, salt, and pepper in a large bowl. Add beans and toss to combine.

Arrange beans in a single layer in a large heavy roasting pan. Roast 10 minutes. Turn and roast 5 minutes, until beans are crisp-tender. Transfer to a bowl; garnish with walnuts. Serve warm.

Serves 4

NOTE: Roast walnuts in a pie pan in oven with beans 2 to 3 minutes, until aromatic and browned.

CHERRY TOMATOES WITH FETA

1lb cherry tomatoes
2 tablespoons olive oil
2 tablespoons chopped fresh flat-leaf parsley
2 tablespoons chopped fresh basil
1 large clove garlic, minced
1/2 cup (2oz) crumbled feta
salt and freshly ground pepper, to taste

Preheat oven to 400F (205C). Combine tomatoes, oil, herbs, and garlic in a large heavy roasting pan. Stir to combine, coating tomatoes with oil and seasoning.

Roast about 5 minutes, or until tomatoes are hot and shiny (do not roast until skins split). Remove from the oven.

Add feta to tomatoes and toss to combine. Roast about 3 minutes more, or until feta is softened. Season with salt and pepper (feta is salty so go easy on salt). Serve warm or at room temperature as a side dish, as part of a salad, or with toasted French bread.

Serves 4

SICILIAN OLIVES

1lb mixed green and black olives
1 tablespoon olive oil
1 large clove garlic, sliced
$^1/_2$ teaspoon dried oregano
$^1/_2$ teaspoon dried rosemary
1 teaspoon coarsely ground black pepper
shredded zest of 1 lemon
2 tablespoons fresh lemon juice

Preheat oven to 475F (245C). Drain olives and pat dry with paper towels.

Toss the olives, olive oil, garlic, oregano, rosemary, and pepper in a medium bowl. Transfer to a large heavy baking sheet.

Roast 5 to 10 minutes, until hot and aromatic. Transfer to a bowl and toss with lemon zest and lemon juice. Serve warm

Makes about 3 cups

— SLOW-ROASTED TOMATOES —

3lb tomatoes
2 cloves garlic, sliced (optional)
salt and freshly ground pepper
1 to 2 tablespoons olive oil

Preheat oven to 450F (230C). Cut tomatoes in half crosswise. Squeeze out some of the seeds and juice.

Arrange tomatoes, cut sides up, in one layer in a large heavy roasting pan. Sprinkle garlic (if using) over tomatoes. Season with salt and pepper. Drizzle olive oil over tomatoes.

Roast about 1 hour, until juices have evaporated and tomatoes just begin to brown on the edges. Roasting time will depend on the type of tomato and how much juice the tomatoes contain.

Serves 4

—— PEA PODS & MUSHROOMS ——

1lb sugar snap peas
8oz small button mushrooms
1 tablespoon peanut oil
1 tablespoon soy sauce
1 tablespoon grated fresh ginger
1 teaspoon sugar
1 clove garlic, minced

Preheat oven to 500F (260C). Remove ends and any strings from peas. Quickly rinse mushrooms in cold water and pat dry. Trim stems even with caps.

Combine oil, soy sauce, ginger, sugar, and garlic in a bowl. Add peas and mushrooms and toss to combine.

Arrange vegetables in a single layer in a large heavy roasting pan. Roast 5 minutes. Turn and roast 5 minutes, until juices evaporate and peas are crisp-tender.

Serves 4

RUSTIC TOMATO SAUCE

1 sweet onion, roasted (page 87)
2lb tomatoes, roasted (page 82)
2 tablespoons chopped fresh basil, or 1 tablespoon
  dried
1 cup beef or vegetable stock
salt and freshly ground pepper, to taste

Place onion in a food processor. Pulse until coarsely chopped.

Add tomatoes and basil and pulse until chopped but not pureed; leave some texture.

Transfer mixture to a saucepan over medium heat. Add stock; bring to a boil. Reduce heat and simmer to desired consistency. Serve with pasta.

Makes about 2 cups

—— SWEET ONION FLOWERS ——

4 large (about 12oz) sweet onions
4 tablespoons olive oil
4 tablespoon balsamic vinegar
2 teaspoons chopped fresh thyme, or $^3/_4$ teaspoon
  dried
salt and freshly ground pepper, to taste

Preheat oven to 450F (230C). Peel onions; trim root ends so onions are flat. Using a large knife, cut each onion into quarters, cutting to within $^1/_2$ inch of the bottom. Cut each quarter into 4 wedges.

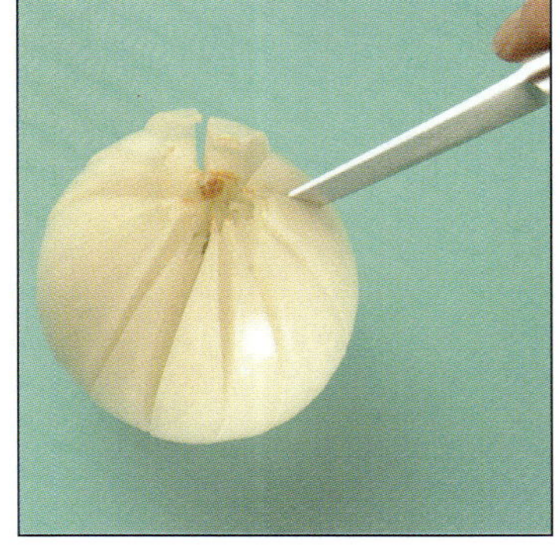

Place onions in a large heavy roasting pan. Using your fingers, slightly open onions.

Combine oil, vinegar, and thyme in a small bowl. Drizzle over onions, spooning mixture between layers. Season with salt and pepper. Roast in bottom third of oven about 30 minutes, until onions still hold their shapes and are just tender. Using a wide spatula, transfer onions to a serving plate.

Serves 8

——— RUB VARIATIONS ———

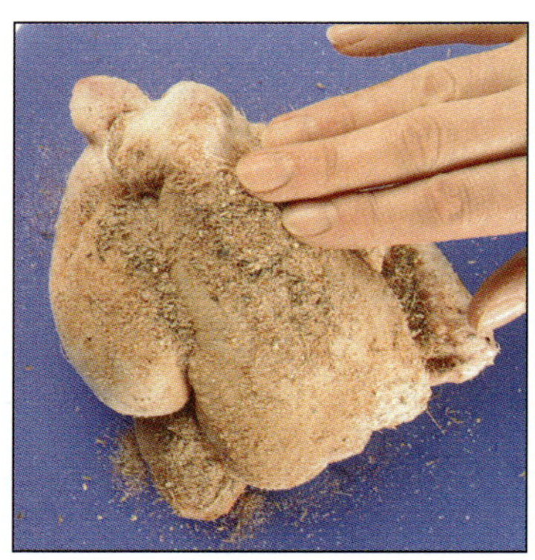

SPICY CAJUN RUB

1/4 cup sweet paprika
4 teaspoons freshly ground black pepper
2 teaspoons dried thyme
2 teaspoons garlic powder
2 teaspoons sugar
1 teaspoon cayenne pepper, or to taste
1 teaspoon salt, or to taste

Combine all ingredients in a small bowl. To use, remove small amounts with a spoon and rub into chicken, fish or steak with your fingers.

Stored in a tightly closed container, the rub will keep up to 6 months.

Makes about 1/2 cup; enough for 2 chickens or 4 to 6 steaks

SOUTHWESTERN RUB

2 tablespoons light brown sugar
1 tablespoon salt
1 tablespoon ground allspice
1 teaspoon ground ginger
1 teaspoon freshly ground black pepper
1 teaspoon garlic powder
1/2 teaspoon ground nutmeg
1/2 teaspoon ground cinnamon
1/2 teaspoon ground cloves
1 teaspoon hot chile powder or cayenne pepper, or to taste

Combine all ingredients in a small bowl.

To use, remove small amounts with a spoon and rub into pork, beef, or chicken with your fingers. Stored in a tightly closed container, the rub will keep up to 6 months.

Makes about 1/3 cup; enough for 1 chicken or 1 small roast.

JERK RUB

1/2 cup mild or medium chile powder
1 tablespoon hot chile powder (optional)
1 tablespoon ground cumin
1 tablespoon ground coriander
1 tablespoon salt
1 tablespoon sugar
1 tablespoon dried oregano

Combine all ingredients in a small bowl. To use, remove small amounts with a spoon and rub into pork, beef or chicken with your fingers.

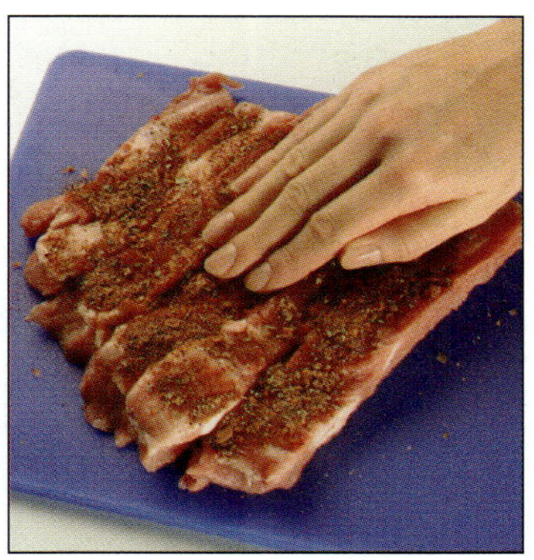

Stored in a tightly closed container, the rub will keep up to 6 months.

Makes about 3/4 cup; enough for 3 chickens or a large roast

CARAMELIZED APPLES

4 medium Braeburn, McIntosh, or Golden Delicious
  apples
2 tablespoons butter
1/4 cup plus 1 tablespoon sugar
1 teaspoon ground cinnamon
1/2 teaspoon ground mace
1/4 teaspoon ground cloves
whipped cream or ice cream, to serve

Preheat oven to 450F (230C). Peel and core apples. Cut each apple into quarters; cut each quarter into 4 wedges.

Melt butter in a heavy 9-inch skillet over medium heat. Add 1/4 cup sugar; cook, stirring, until bubbly and starting to brown.

Carefully arrange apples wedges around side of hot skillet, slightly overlapping, in concentric circles. Combine spices and 1 tablespoon sugar; sprinkle over apples. Transfer to the oven; roast about 20 minutes, until apples are tender and caramelized. (Depending on the apples, they may be too juicy at this stage. If they are, return to the stove top and boil until juices are thickened.) Serve with whipped cream.

Serves 4–6

– PEARS, BRIE, & CHERRY SAUCE –

2 firm-ripe Comice or Bartlett pears (about 8oz
  each)
1 tablespoon almond oil
4 to 6oz Brie
4 tablespoons slivered almonds, roasted (see Note
  below)
CHERRY SAUCE:
3/4 cup apple juice
1/2 cup port or red wine
1/3 cup chopped dried sweet cherries
1 teaspoon cornstarch mixed with 2 tablespoons
  water

Preheat oven to 450F (230C). Spray a non-stick heavy baking sheet with cooking spray.

To make sauce, combine juice, port, and cherries in a small saucepan over medium heat. Simmer until cherries are softened. Stir in cornstarch mixture; cook, stirring, until slightly thickened. Cut each pear into halves; remove cores with a melon baler. Place a pear half, cut side down, on a work surface. Starting near the stem end, cut each half into thin slices, leaving slices attached at the stem end and following the contours of the pears. Transfer pears to prepared baking sheet with a spatula. Fan pears slightly; lightly brush with almond oil.

Roast about 20 minutes, until tender. Using a large spatula, transfer pear halves to 4 warmed plates. Divide Brie over pears. Sprinkle with almonds and serve warm with sauce on the side.

Serves 4

NOTE: Roast almonds alongside pears for about 3 minutes.

– PINEAPPLE & VANILLA BUTTER –

1 small pineapple
1/4 cup mild honey
2 tablespoons butter
2 teaspoons pure vanilla extract
vanilla ice cream (optional)

Preheat oven to 500F (260C). Remove pineapple crown by slicing a thin piece off the top; cut pineapple into quarters. With a flexible knife, cut the fruit from the shell and remove to a cutting board. Cut crosswise into about 5 equal pieces. Return the pieces to the shells, staggering the pieces.

Heat the honey and butter in a small saucepan until butter melts. Stir in vanilla extract.

Place the pineapple on a large heavy baking sheet. Brush some of honey mixture over the pineapple. Roast about 10 minutes, until slightly browned on the edges. Brush with remaining honey mixture and serve warm with ice cream on the side if desired.

Serves 4

— BLUEBERRY FILLED PEACHES —

6 peaches
6 teaspoons honey
1 tablespoon almond oil
1 pint fresh blueberries
RASPBERRY SAUCE:
1 (12oz) packet frozen unsweetened raspberries,
  thawed
1/3 cup sugar, or to taste
1 tablespoon fresh lemon juice

Preheat oven to 500F (260C). Bring a pot of water to a boil. Add peaches; boil about 1 minute. Immediately transfer to ice water to cool.

Peel peaches; cut into halves. Remove pits and enlarge holes with a melon baller. Arrange peaches, cut sides up, in a large heavy roasting pan. Add 1 teaspoon honey to each peach. Lightly drizzle with almond oil. Roast about 10 minutes, until peaches are hot and lightly cooked.

Combine raspberries, sugar, and lemon juice in a food processor. Pulse until pureed. Strain out seeds, if desired. Spoon pools of sauce on dessert plates; place 2 peach halves on each plate. Fill peaches with blueberries.

Serves 6

FIGS WITH HONEY

8 large fresh figs
1/2 cup balsamic vinegar
1/2 cup honey
1 teaspoon almond oil
1/2 cup (4oz) cream cheese, softened
1 tablespoon powdered sugar
1/4 teaspoon pure almond extract

Preheat oven to 500F (260C). Cut figs from stem ends almost to blossom end, leaving halves attached. Arrange figs on a non-stick heavy baking sheet.

Combine vinegar, honey, and oil in a small skillet. Boil until reduced by about one-third. Drizzle about half of the honey mixture over figs. Roast 10 minutes, until softened and glazed.

Meanwhile, combine cream cheese, sugar, and almond extract in a small bowl. Shape into 8 balls, using about 1 tablespoon cheese mixture for each. Arrange figs on a serving plate. Place a cheese ball in center of each fig. Drizzle remaining honey mixture over stuffed figs; serve immediately.

Serves 4

— CHERRY-STUFFED APPLES —

1 cup dried sweet dark cherries, chopped
1 to 2 tablespoons maraschino liqueur or kirsch
4 large apples, such as Braeburn or MacIntosh
4 tablespoons honey
1 teaspoon ground cinnamon
1/2 cup apple juice, white wine or water
cinnamon-topped whipped cream, to serve

Preheat oven to 375F (180C). Combine cherries and liqueur in a small bowl. Wash apples in cold water and dry. Remove apple cores. With a knife, make a cut through the skin around the center of each apple to help prevent bursting.

Arrange apples in a baking dish. Stuff apples with cherries, packing the cherries firmly into cavities. Pour any remaining liqueur over apples. Drizzle honey over apples and sprinkle with cinnamon.

Pour apple juice around apples. Bake apples about 45 minutes, until soft. Serve hot or at room temperature with whipped cream.

Serves 4

INDEX